DRUMCREE

by
John A. Pickering
RECTOR 1983-2007

AMBASSADOR INTERNATIONAL
Greenville, South Carolina • Belfast, Northern Ireland

DRUMCREE

ISBN 978-1-84030-212-7

Ambassador Publications
a division of
Ambassador Productions Ltd.
Providence House
Ardenlee Street,
Belfast,
BT6 8QJ
Northern Ireland
www.ambassador-productions.com

Emerald House
427 Wade Hampton Blvd.
Greenville
SC 29609, USA
www.emeraldhouse.com

DEDICATION

To SARAH, my daughter, who worked very hard with me as I wrote this book.

And to the memory of OLIVE my wife, who always knew how difficult it would be for me to write this book.

"Be still and know that I am God."

Psalm 46:10

Acknowledgements

I would like to thank most sincerely all the people who have helped me immensely to write this book. Without their help I could not have accomplished this task.

I am so grateful to my typists for being so longsuffering and extremely patient as I re-worked my script many times. I am in a deep debt of gratitude to them for the many hours they spent typing my script. The people I refer to are my daughter Sarah Cordner, along with my friends, Kathryn Anderson, Elizabeth Cochrane, Gretta Grimason, Pauline McClelland, Daphne Morrow and Wendy Walsh.

The reading of my script and the making of many helpful changes before completion was carried out painstakingly for me by my friend Phyllis Harrison, who spent innumerable hours doing invaluable work for which I am so grateful.

I express my gratitude to those who provided me with photographs by courtesy, David Jones LOL No. 1, Alan Lewis/Photopress, Belfast Telegraph, News Letter, Portadown Times, Press Association, Portadown LOL No. 1 and the Irish Times for their map as well as LOL No. 1 for their motif.

I am most grateful to Sam Lowry, and all the staff at Ambassador Publications for making this publication possible.

There were a number of other people who helped me to whom I extend my great thanks.

John A. Pickering
Portadown, Craigavon
14th May, 2009

Drumcree - Portadown
Northern Ireland

New York Times with slight amendment

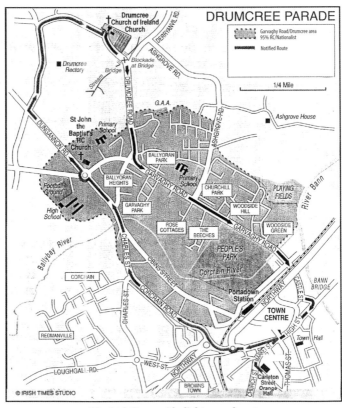

The Irish Times with slight amendments

List of Contents

Introduction

ONE evening, while watching some video footage about the early years of protest at Drumcree when Portadown District LOL No 1 were prevented from parading along Garvaghy Road after their annual attendance at worship in Drumcree Parish Church, I wondered aloud to my wife Olive, about how many people properly understood the Drumcree situation and all the events that had occurred during those momentous weeks in July each year from 1995.

I recalled my former history teacher Mr Henderson, telling my class in Omagh Academy that Bismarck had once commented about the "German Unity Question" in the nineteenth century, "There were only three people who understood our problems. One was Napoleon III, who is dead, the second was Frederick William IV of Prussia, who has gone mad, and I am the third person, but I have forgotten all about it". At Drumcree I saw history repeating itself.

I pointed out to Olive how many of those who were present at Drumcree in those early days had since died, and a number of people throughout the whole country certainly said and did many mad things, while I wish I had never known about those events and indeed would like to be able to forget them!

However, I cannot forget. What happened was only too real and had such serious consequences that I have decided I must write about it. I am glad that at the time I took detailed notes about the events of each day and night since the July service of 1995. As part of my records I filed away all relevant newspaper cuttings, recorded radio reports and videoed hours of television coverage.

This is not a thorough account of absolutely everything which took place, as so much is already well documented. It would be impossible to put everything on record as so much happened, much of it behind the scenes. Also there were some hidden agendas, and unpleasant double think. And spin was invented. Perhaps as Dean Godson says about the entire peace process "the full story will probably never be told."

My purpose is to share my personal experiences as the clergyman of Drumcree Parish, describing what I saw and heard, what I did and what I tried to accomplish. Not being a member of the Orange Order gave me an advantage in being a middle man in the situation.

When the Drumcree dispute was ongoing naturally I became involved with the issue of the civil rights of the members of the Orange Order to parade and to protest against what was known as the re-routing, but which was effectively a ban on the parade, which was very distressing to the Order as parading is seen as the most telling way for it to show its Protestant identity. Neil Jarmin says that parading is, "a popular expression of cultural identity and difference".[1] There was also the right to protest against the parade by the Garvaghy Road Residents' Coalition (GRRC) formerly known as the Garvaghy Road Residents' Group. However, the dispute developed into much more than that. In Northern Ireland for some time the majority Protestant and unionist section and the minority Roman Catholic and nationalist section had been feeling threatened by each other. As a result the stand-off which took place between the Orange Order and the GRRC provided the occasion for a visible expression of the feelings of these two sections, and the drawing of the proverbial line in the sand.

However, where I became really deeply involved was in the question of religious rights, especially in the matter of the right of public worship of Almighty God. People

1.   N. Jarmin, "Material Conflicts" (Oxford 1997) p 56

were distressed with their civil liberties being curtailed and then were aghast that their religious liberties might be restricted. When efforts were made to deny people that right I stood firm on this issue and I am glad I was able to bring Orangemen and everyone else the assurance of their right to public worship at all times.

As I write about my experiences at Drumcree I want to show that my role was always that of a pastor to people in need and to witness to how God gave me, my wife Olive and daughter Sarah the strength to cope with the situation, as God can help anyone in any circumstances, if they trust in him. No matter how desperate a situation may have seemed there was always a strong hope for a better day, a feeling of assurance of better days ahead.

PART ONE

Background

Background

To set all the events in context I have included background information about myself, the Parish of Drumcree, the Orange Order and the history of the Orange Parade Services at Drumcree.

Chapter 1
My Background

THE name "Pickering" was known at the Battle of the Boyne in 1690, as King William III of the House of Orange had among his army men called Pickering. Later they settled near Castledawson, Co. Londonderry.

About two hundred and fifty years later, during the middle of the Second World War, on Easter Sunday 13th April 1941 about 2.00am I was born, as a successor to one of those soldiers of King William and destined I believe, for a crisis period in Drumcree beginning in 1995, over fifty years after my birth.

In those days, as the custom was, I was born at home, which was 5 Dublin Road, Omagh. The area was known as Dublin Road corner.[1] Later I lived at different places in the town and area.

Those who know me from my early days will remember my father James[2] and my mother Selina, who ran a confectionery business next door to at No. 3. My brother James was born in 1943. I attended Omagh Academy from 1945 until 1959. One of the earliest memories I can recall was VE Day in 1945, standing outside the YMCA watching soldiers parade past, after the trying years of the War, but then life began to improve. I was not the most robust of children and suffered often from illness. One of my vivid early memories was of 16 May 1951 when there was a large loyalist demonstration in Omagh to protest against any move to include Tyrone & Fermanagh in the Irish Republic. The demonstration had as its slogan "Ulster is British".

In those days I belonged to the Methodist Church and from my early years I was a keen admirer of the Rev. John Wesley, which led to me joining the Church of Ireland. I was converted to Christ on 18th February 1955, at a Youth for Christ meeting addressed by the Rev. Dr. John Wesley White, who was later an associate evangelist of Dr. Billy Graham.

---

1. On Saturday 15th August 1998 at 3.10 pm the dreadful bomb of death and injury that had been planted in Omagh exploded just around the corner from where I was born. One of the 29 people and unborn twins who were murdered, was Sean McGrath with whom I used to play at that corner fifty years before.

2. Haldane Mitchell, "Images of Omagh" (2000) Vol 8 p 59
"Clergy of Derry and Raphoe" (1999) - D W Crooks

My family travelled to New Zealand and stayed for a short time at the end of the 1950's. Upon return my family settled in Enniskillen and I went up to Magee University College, Londonderry to study Arts and then to Trinity College, University of Dublin, to continue my course from where I graduated with a BA in 1963, (MA in 1966), then trained for the ministry of the Church of Ireland, and was ordained in 1965.[3]

I served in Magheralin as curate from 1965-1967 under the Rev P. J. Synnott. I found it to be a great parish with many people and much activity, so I greatly enjoyed my ministry there.

Then I was in Ballinamore, Co Leitrim from 1967-1971, first as a Bishop's Curate and later as rector, being in charge of my own parish, which I appreciated greatly.

After that I went to the Hibernian Bible Society based in Dublin as Deputation Secretary from 1971–1974, where I found more challenge and had the great experience of travelling throughout the Republic promoting the Bible.

Following that I was in Cootehill, Co. Cavan from 1974-1980, during which time I married Olive née Young of Limerick on 15th May 1975 and our daughter Sarah was born on 19th March 1976. I found my approach to ministry was largely not accepted there. In 1979 Olive was diagnosed with cancer which was a dreadful experience. That was a very dark time, but thank God, Olive recovered.

---

3. Armagh Clergy" (2000) – W.E.C. Fleming
   "Clergy of Down and Dromore" (1996) - F. Rankin (Ed.)
   "Clergy of Kilmore, Elphin and Ardagh" (2008) – D. W. Crooks

Next I was rector of the Keady Group of parishes from 1980-1983. It was a great pleasure to be there even though my time was short.

I was appointed Rector of Drumcree in October 1983, a parish with a history and challenges during my early days, but with supportive people. Half of my years at Drumcree were taken up with the Drumcree dispute, but I know that I was called by God, to be there. I found it so much better to be minister in a parish with just one church, with a large group of parishioners and with finance provided honestly.

While at Drumcree, sadly Olive died on Easter Sunday 16th April 2006 from the return of cancer. I remained at Drumcree for the rest of my full-time ministry of over forty-two years, until I retired on 30th September 2007.

Chapter 2
The Parish of Drumcree

THE PARISH - EARLY YEARS

THE Parish of Drumcree[1] is situated on the northern side of Portadown, Northern Ireland. In my research of the parish I discovered that the name Drumcree comes from old Irish sources, deriving from "Drumcribh"[2] (pronounced Drumcreeve), which denotes "Ridge of the Branch", that is the ridge upon which the branchy trees grew. Drumcree may have been an early centre of Druid worship. As a Christian centre, Drumcree is thought to

---

1. I. Carrick, 'Historical Sketch of Drumcree' (1991)
2. Another spelling is Droim Cri meaning boundary ridge. (See Ulster Place Names)

date back to Celtic times. It was once possessed by the Culdees of Armagh, who were formed about the sixth century, to oversee the services of the Cathedral, and presumably the whole area. By 1111 parishes were formed in the Irish Church, and Drumcree consisted of sixty-six townlands stretching from Muckery to Ballyworkan. Researching further I found many interesting historical facts. The Irish Church including Drumcree Parish, came under the authority of the Church of Rome in 1172 and remained so until the Reformation in 1536, after which it was called The Church of Ireland. Those who did not wish to convert formed the Roman Catholic Church.

THE CHURCH BUILDING

All the churches at Drumcree are believed to have been on the site of the present church.

A map prepared in 1609, shows the ruins of a church in Drumcree Churchyard. It appears that a church was built on the present site shortly after the Ulster Plantation in 1610. It was "a plain stone building, rough cast and white-washed", and had a gallery. It seated 500 people and the usual attendance was around 400.

It was proposed by Oliver Cromwell about 1657 that Drumcree Church and Seagoe Church should be demolished and a new church built at Edenderry, but this suggestion was never implemented.

A Chapel-of-Ease was established in Portadown in 1826 for the Parish of Portadown, which was formed in

1824 by the separation of thirteen townlands from Drumcree.

In the mid 1850's it was decided to replace the church with a new one. The foundation stone of the replacement church at Drumcree, which is the present church building, was laid in the Chancel on Ascension Day, Thursday 17th May 1855, hence the reason for the dedication, "The Church of the Ascension".

The church, which now stands almost on the site of the previous church, was consecrated on Tuesday, 28th October 1856 by the Bishop of Down, Dromore and Connor, Robert Bent Knox. The only part of the old church which is incorporated into the present church is the tower and spire. Weddings were held in the porch during the building of the church.

A War Memorial for the First World War was erected in 1921 and in 1989 another Memorial was erected to commemorate those who died in the Second World War.

The Chancel mosaic tiles and steps were put in place in 1955 in memory of Rev. F. J. Halahan and the church was re-roofed in 1991.

THE PARISH - LATER YEARS

The Rev. John Wesley had a profound influence upon the parish and visited it six times between 1769 and 1785 and preached at Derryanvil. The religious revival of 1859, which swept the north of Ireland, is known to have brought a great spiritual awakening in Drumcree.

Five more townlands were separated from Drumcree in 1867 to help form the Parish of Diamond, namely Corglass, Annagora, Ballymakeown, Coharra and Cushenny. Drumcree has therefore ever since contained forty-eight townlands.

Up to 1870 the Church of Ireland was supported by the State, but as only one in eight of the population belonged to the Church of Ireland the State ceased to provide for it. The Irish Church Act of 1869 brought the Disestablishment of the Church of Ireland from 1st January 1871. This meant that the Church of Ireland lost millions of pounds and much property. Drumcree lost nearly all its five-hundred-and-sixty-five acres of Glebe Land. There was some compensation but much generosity was shown by the laity and clergy, and so the future was faced with confidence.

Church Halls at Richmount, Breagh, Derrycory and Derryall were established in the nineteenth and early twentieth centuries. The Churchyard was extended in 1901 and 1922 while the Parochial Hall was built in 1902. The present rectory was built in 1964, replacing the previous one built in 1827.

The centenary of the Parochial Hall was celebrated in 2007 by being refurbished and by having the ancillary halls completely reconstructed all at a cost of £650,000. On Saturday 16th June 2007 a Dedication Ceremony was performed by me, while my daughter Sarah performed the Opening Ceremony. To mark the occasion a tablet was provided by the Mothers' Union in memory of my wife Olive.

Rectors 1781-2007

1781-1804 George Maunsell: one of the founders of the Orange Order.

1804-1826 Stewart Blacker

1826-1870 Charles Alexander

1870-1879 Robert Hamilton

1879-1883 William Twibill

1883-1890 Andrew Leitch: District Master of Portadown LOL No 1 1886-1891

1890-1900 Frederick Austin, Chaplain to Portadown LOL No 1

1900-1904 Edward Crowe

1905-1948 Francis Halahan

1948-1961 Robert Dennis

1961-1983 John Ford

1983-2007 John Pickering

Chapter 3
The Orange Order

FOR those not familiar with the Orange Order I feel it is appropriate to outline a brief history of the Order so that the Drumcree situation can be more clearly understood. As is well known the roots of the Orange Order go back to William, Prince of the Protestant House of Orange in Holland, in the late seventeenth century.

At that time in Europe the despotism of Louis XIV of France, who was aligned with the Roman Catholic King James II of the British Isles, was challenged by the central and northern countries of Europe including Austria,

Spain, Sweden, Denmark, Bavaria, Prussia, a number of German states, Holland and the Vatican with Pope Innocent II, who formed themselves into the League of Augsburg, which was led by William.

William III   *Schomberg House*

The most decisive battle in the struggle was the Battle of the Boyne which was fought at the River Boyne on 1st July 1690, when William defeated James at what was the biggest battle ever fought in the British Isles. It was the largest in terms of numbers involved but there were only about 1,500 deaths. The victory brought great celebration throughout Europe, including Vienna, where the Te Deum was sung in the Roman Catholic Cathedral. Although it has been the custom to celebrate the victory of a battle the day after it was won, since 1752 the victory of the battle was celebrated on 12th July, because eleven days were added to the calendar then. Union Jacks are hoisted at many churches on 1st July, the day of the battle.

After this victory civil and religious liberty was guaranteed for everyone, a fact which is now recognised in the Irish Republic, by a Boyne Heritage Centre being established at the site of the battle. James II was replaced on the throne by William and Mary and so absolute monarchy was replaced by constitutional democracy. The Glorious Revolution of 1688 was celebrated and the Act of Settlement established.

Soon many Orange societies were formed in Ireland and England such as The Loyal and Friendly Society of the Blue and Orange, the numerous Boyne Clubs and the Royal Boyne Society.

Later violent Protestant agrarian groups were formed, such as The Peep O'Day Boys and Thrashers, and violent Roman Catholic agrarian societies were also set up because of disputes over land between Protestants and Roman Catholics. These disputes culminated in a confrontation at the Diamond, in Co. Armagh near Dan Winter's cottage on 21st September 1795 between Protestants and the Roman Catholic Defenders, where the Defenders were defeated in a short battle. Immediately afterwards, because of the similarity between the Battle of the Boyne and the Battle of the Diamond, it was decided to form an Orange society to help to defend Protestantism, which soon became called the Loyal Orange Institution of Ireland. Many of the members of the pre-existing Orange societies became officers and members. While some Peep O'Day Boys joined the Orange Order, "they found themselves in a markedly different association", as Mervyn Jess says in his book,[1] because they found it was a peaceful organisation.

The Rev. S. Cupples, Grand Master of Co. Antrim, writing in 1799, disclaimed any connection between the Orange Order and The Peep O'Day Boys,[2] because it did not want any connection with violence.

Typical Banner   *David Jones*

1   Mervyn Jess, "The Orange Order" (O'Brien Press 2007) p18
2   A. McClelland, "The Formation of the Orange Order" p2

The Orange Order spread rapidly. Portadown District LOL No. 1 was formed in 1796 and grew to thirty four lodges, of which eight were in the Drumcree area. By May 1798 the Orange Order had become established in almost every county in Ireland. The members met in lodges, which were represented in district lodges and in turn in county lodges and then in Grand Lodge. Parading, while wearing sashes, was the chief way the Orange gave expression to its ideals and this increased in importance as the years passed, with the parades being headed by the carrying of banners, bannerettes and flags and accompanied by music. Parades took various forms, which are now very familiar. There are parades on the 12th July to a number of venues. It is also always the custom for a lodge to have a short parade following the unfurling of a new banner or some other special occasion. Then there are the church parades, to attend what is commonly known as Orange Services, normally held on the Sunday before the Twelfth or the most suitable Sunday in July or even June. I call these services Orange Parade Services, that is services to which Orangemen parade.

Each Orange lodge meets monthly and takes the form of a Bible reading, prayers and a general meeting where current issues are discussed. There are also women's lodges and junior lodges.

Politically, the Orange Order has had a close association with the Ulster Unionist Party (UUP), even from before the partition of Northern Ireland from the rest of Ireland in 1921. The nationalists resented this association, especially during the period of the Stormont Government 1921-1972, when the Ulster Unionist Party was the majority party.

The Orange Order has grown into an international organisation and is active in Europe, Australasia, North America and Africa.

The Orange Order has always seen itself as a fraternity of Protestants meeting to have dinners and concerts, along with providing charity through The Lord Enniskillen Memorial Orange Orphan Society. Recently the Orange Order has become increasingly associated with the Ulster-Scots movement and the culture that it represents and promotes at home and overseas.

Chapter 4

Drumcree Orange Parade Services 1807-1994

THE EARLY YEARS

SHORTLY after becoming Rector of Drumcree I enquired about the origin of the Orange Parade Services at Drumcree and elsewhere. I learnt that Orangemen had been attending services at Drumcree from about the time of the formation of the Orange Order at the Diamond in 1795 and Portadown in 1796. In those days I understand, the various trade guilds attended Church services on a particular day each year, so the Orangemen decided to do likewise, having indeed a good reason for doing so, as the

Orange Order was a Protestant religious organisation. The day chosen was in July, when the Battle of the Boyne in 1690 is celebrated.

At that time the Parish Church for the whole Portadown area was at Drumcree, so members of the Portadown District established the practice of parading to Drumcree Church. The church parade was always without banners, and without music until the 1950's. The parade came from Portadown via Obins Street also called 'the Tunnel area' and returned by Garvaghy Road, also called 'the walk'.

Plowden records that a Rev. Devine preached at a service on Drumcree on 1st July in 1795, before the formation of the Orange Institution. Unruly behaviour is said to have taken place afterwards, but Plowden was unfavourable to Orangeism.[1] William Henry Wolsey records that after the formation of Portadown District LOL No. 1 in 1796 Orangemen went to Drumcree in 1807 to hear a sermon by the rector the Rev Stewart Blacker.[2] That was on Monday 12th July. It was the first recorded service after the formation of the Orange Order in 1795. Wolsey also records that the Orange attended a service in 1822.

There was a period between 1823 and 1833, except 1831, when the Orange attended services at Drumcree on 5th November each year.[3] Although Orange

1   F. Plowden, "Orange Societies" (Coyne 1810, Schomberg House Library) p 17
2   W. H. Wolsey, "Orangeism in Portadown District" (1935), p6
3   W. H. Wolsey, p 7

demonstrations were banned by an act of Parliament in 1832 (The Party Processions Act), nevertheless the Orangemen attended church. It is recorded that on Sunday 12th July 1835 "A number of the Orangemen in the town and neighbourhood assembled and walked in procession to Drumcree Church where an eloquent sermon was delivered by the Rev C. Alexander. The procession was not distinguished by either music or flags, nor did it exhibit any insignia of the order, except for a few who wore Orange scarves. After the conclusion of the sermon the Orangemen returned to their respective homes in that quiet, peaceable and orderly way in which they left the town and everything passed off amicably, not the slightest disturbance having occurred or any breach of the peace committed."[4]

Wolsey refers to other services attended by Orangemen. There is a reference in the Drumcree Parish Preachers' Books to the attendance at a service in 1846.

While I found these references to Orangemen attending services, I cannot prove attendance every year since 1807. Yet it is still a long time since Orangemen of Portadown District began attending in 1807. But attendance seems to have become more established from 1857 when the present church, The Church of the Ascension, was built. The church, being bigger was able to accommodate a larger number of worshippers and so the Orange Parade Services seemed to have become greater occasions.

---

4   "Newry Telegraph" quoted by W. H. Wolsey p 9

From 1857 the Orange Order attended the service every July except in 1987, although on that occasion there was a token presence of Orangemen. The Preachers' Books, which names the preacher at every service, includes a record of the number of worshippers every July since 1857 along with the amount of the collection and to which charity it was given. Some years the attendance was very large, as on Sunday 12th July 1885 and Sunday 10th July 1887 when 2,500 attended each service. To have all this information for over one hundred and fifty years is to know that there has been a long and great tradition of the Orangemen of Portadown attending services in Drumcree Parish Church.[5]

Drumcree Church in early 1900's   *David Jones*

---

5   During July some years there was a certain amount of unrest, but it appears to have been on weekdays and not Sundays.

THE EARLY TWENTIETH CENTURY

At the beginning of the 1900s Sunday 9th July 1916 was a particularly sad day because the Battle of the Somme had so recently begun, at which 300 men of the 9th Royal Irish Fusiliers, 36th Ulster Division from County Armagh and County Monaghan were killed on the first day, 1st July, among them Drumcree parishioners Frederick Woods of Derrybrughas and William Wylie of Derryall. Ever since that, the Battle of the Somme has been remembered with much poignancy at the Orange Parade Services in July every year.

As the 1900's continued, apart from the occasional disquiet, the parades continued without hindrance and indeed with good numbers. Attendance at the services continued during World War I and World War II, but there were no parades during the years 1940 to 1944.[6] The parades for many years appeared to have been well received by the nationalist community, with residents of Obins Street sitting along the footpath observing those on parade. Reggie Telford, 82, who has been parading for fifty years says, "Catholics and parades, the Catholics didn't care. The older ones would shout out at you, You're looking well this morning and the like. There was no animosity and or anything like that." Yvonne Sterritt, a Catholic I know well told the Belfast Telegraph, "As a child I went out to see the Orangemen and enjoyed the fun on the eleventh night."[7]

6   R. E. Jones and others, "The Orange Citadel" (1996), Appendix 2
7   11 July 1995

THE LATER TWENTIETH CENTURY

However, when the 1980's approached some opposition was expressed to the parades proceeding along Obins Street[8] on the outward journey. This was heightened by the loyalist objection to a St Patrick's Day parade on Park Road in 1985. In July 1985 it was declared by the RUC that the Orange parade would not be permitted into Obins Street. However that decision was reversed the day before the parade, to allow it to proceed. So the parade took place on Sunday 7th July 1985 with 1,500 attending. The preacher was Rev. Roy Boyd, a former curate of the parish, while I conducted the service.

The parade on Sunday 6th July 1986 was allowed through Obins Street, but it was delayed in getting through because the Orangemen objected to the RUC preventing a Mr George Seawright of Belfast from parading. Nearly 1,500 Orangemen were on parade that year.

The 1987 parade scheduled for Sunday 5th July did not take place, because it was not permitted to enter Woodhouse Street, leading to Obins Street and Orangemen did not wish to accept this ruling. Later they dispersed after a short service in the town centre. The normal Sunday Service at Drumcree was also held with approximately 100 Orangemen attending the service.

---

8   Obins Street became inhabited mainly by Roman Catholic people, the Protestants having left the area gradually over a number of years. Also Obins Street was no longer a direct route into Portadown since the building of the Northway road.

From 1988 the outward journey was re-routed from Obins Street to Northway. The Orange Order accepted the re-routing reluctantly and continued to attend the service at Drumcree and to follow the traditional route back to Carleton Street via Garvaghy Road, where there were usually some mild but lawful protests. This was still the situation in 1994.

PART TWO

The Years of Protest

Chapter 5
1995 Drumcree One

AS 1995 approached strong opposition to the parade on the Garvaghy Road began to be expressed by the residents who had formed the GRRC. Their chairman was Mr Brendan McKenna a new resident to the area, who had been imprisoned for his involvement in a bomb attack on the Royal British Legion Hall in Portadown in August 1981. Spokesmen were Rev Eamon Stack S.J., Rev Brian Lennon S.J. and Mr Joe Duffy.

The GRRC wanted to talk with the Portadown District LOL No 1 before a walk (a parade). However the Orange Order said they would only talk after a walk, because they did not want to be seen to be asking GRRC's permission to walk. Listening to the media reports about the opposition I found that the residents objected to the parade going through the Garvaghy Road because the population had changed from being mostly Protestant in the 1960's when most of the houses were built, to becoming mostly Roman Catholic by the 1990's.

They felt that a parade of Orangemen, in an area which was inhabited by mainly Roman Catholic people was demeaning and domineering making the residents feel they were being treated as second class citizens. The residents also claimed that the area was suffering from social deprivation.

I found that the response of the Orangemen was that they fully respected the right of the Garvaghy Road residents to protest and did not want to cause offence to the residents at any time. The Orangemen were keen to minimise any upset by being preceded by only one band of accordions comprising mainly of young girls, playing only hymn tunes. They had also arranged that the parade would be shortened in length, by the Orangemen walking six abreast and passing any point within twelve minutes. The parade was simply one of Orangemen returning to Portadown along Garvaghy Road, which they had first walked in 1807. The road, which is a main arterial road into the town, has few houses actually facing towards the road, as most of the population live in estates set back from the road. In fact most Sundays, at that time, the road is deserted.

Garvaghy Road   *Alan Lewis/Photopress*

Also the Orangemen said that while they were concerned about social deprivation they never saw it as their role to bring about change, as the issue was such a very wide one and required attention from the government. They do not accept that the parade and social economic regeneration of the area should be considered in any kind of relationship to each other.

The Orangemen made me aware of the fact that in the past there had been about ten or more parades in the Drumcree area of the town and that this parade in question was the only one of those parades left (or more accurately about one-third, since only the middle section remains!). So the Orangemen felt strongly that after all their generosity in giving up so many parades at least they should not be prevented from keeping the one remaining parade, which is of such historical and cultural significance. They felt that if they lost the parade on this route and changed their return route from Drumcree it would not be long until objections were made to that route as well and then all their parades would have been suppressed. The journalist, Suzanne Breen, in reflection expressed the situation well by saying, "The Orange Order knows if it capitulates here, then next year demands will be made elsewhere."[1]

Sunday 9th July – Drumcree Sunday

The Morning

As the parade assembled at Carleton Street Orange Hall there was much anxiety, due to the controversy surrounding it because of objections to it by the GRRC. The GRRC wanted to parade from the Garvaghy Road to Carleton Street at 10.00am, but were refused by the Royal Ulster Constabulary (RUC). Sir Hugh Annesley was Chief Constable at the time.

There were about 800 Orangemen on parade which set off shortly after 10.00am, headed by Harold Gracey, Portadown District LOL No 1 District Master, who was soon to become an heroic figure in Orangeism, Denis Watson, Assistant Grand Master of Ireland and David Trimble MP (Upper Bann) a regular attender at this

1   News Letter 2 July 1998

annual service. The parade arrived in good time for attendance at the normal 11.30am service, which was relayed into the Parochial Hall for the overflow of Orangemen and parishioners. I conducted the service and preached the sermon. I said, "Jesus Christ offered the only real hope for the world through personal trust in him. That makes all the difference – Jesus is alive. This hope is what the Orange Order, the Reformation and Christianity is all about. The answer for Northern Ireland and its people is a spiritual renewal." George Robinson, Portadown District LOL No.1 Lay Chaplain read the Lesson and "The Holy City" was sung by Wilson and Wendy Sharpe. The organist was Miss Wendy Henderson.

At the conclusion of the service Harold Gracey thanked me for the serice, as is the custom after all Orange Parade Services.

RUC Cordon   *Belfast Telegraph*

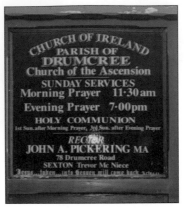

Notice Board

When the parade formed up outside the church for its return to Portadown by its traditional route of Garvaghy Road, to my surprise, as I watched from the churchyard, I saw a cordon of RUC with about six grey land rovers forming a blockade across the road a few yards beyond the bridge down the hill from the church. This was not a good position for the RUC, because there was easy access to the field beyond the bridge. Derryanvil Road was lined on both sides with over forty land rovers.

The RUC informed Harold Gracey and the Officers that the parade would not be permitted to proceed, because there was a group of people who were staging a sit down protest on Garvaghy Road, against the parade. It would not be possible to remove them and let the parade proceed, without public order being disrupted. The Orangemen were shocked to hear this and would not accept that they should be prevented from parading, by a group of people who were unlawfully blocking the road and especially as the parade would not pose any threat to anyone.

So the Orangemen decided to remain at Drumcree until they were permitted to parade along Garvaghy Road. I remember well being near Harold Gracey as he said, "I am for staying". I can still hear his words ringing in my ears as he said, "The brethren of Portadown will not be moving, let it be hours, let it be days, let it be weeks. We are for staying until such times as we can walk our traditional route down the Garvaghy Road."[2]

Gracey appealed to Orangemen from across the Province "to come to Drumcree and show solidarity" with them. So a stand-off was commenced, and a stalemate began.

1641 Drowning   *David Jones*

---

2   News Letter 10 July 1995   Belfast Telegraph 10 July 1995, Irish Times 10 July 1995
       Irish News 10 July 1995, Irish Independent 10 July 1995

The Afternoon

I remember very well David Trimble setting off from the church gate towards the bridge as he took his first physical steps to becoming involved in the Drumcree dispute and a new turn in Northern Ireland politics. Negotiations with Assistant Chief Constable Freddie Hall for the parade to proceed were commenced immediately, helped by Trimble, who was a great strength to LOL No 1.

The Orange established a "headquarters" for themselves in the office in the Parochial Hall to work for a resolution, manned by Stephen McLoughlin, County Armagh LOL Secretary.

If such a situation had been planned a better place could not have been chosen. The 1641 massacre of Protestants by drowning in the River Bann at Portadown has never been forgotten. Portadown is centrally located in the heartland of Orangeism and has been referred to as "the Orange Citadel". The Orange Order was founded at the Diamond, an adjacent parish to Drumcree. Portadown is the No 1 District in Orangeism. It firmly opposed home rule which was regarded as Rome rule. Col. Edward Saunderson MP for North Armagh observed of the Second Home Rule Bill in 1893, "Home Rule may pass this House but it will never pass the bridge at Portadown."[3] And there is a statue to his memory in front of St Mark's Church, Portadown. July being holiday time

---

3   J. R. Whitten (Ed.), "The Millennium Book" (GOLI 2000) p 60
      Dean Godson, "Himself Alone – David Trimble" (Harper 2004) p 100

RUC Riot Squad   Belfast Telegraph

and the weather being very good and an ideal terrain provided excellent conditions for the stand-off.

When news of the impasse was broadcast I was amazed how soon food began to be brought by woman for hungry husbands and boyfriends. An Orangeman undertook to organise the distribution of the refreshments in the Parochial Hall. In a short time he was joined by many women including Elizabeth Cochrane, Lily Boyce, Jean Patterson, Pearl Armstrong and Renee Donaldson. Food was brought from Portadown itself and various places throughout the province. One woman said, "You name it and we are supplied with it. People are bringing it from Dungannon, Aughnacloy and all over."[4] The Parochial Hall quickly became a hive of activity providing

4   News Letter 11 July, 1995

refreshments for brethren day and night, over the days which followed. From then the area at Drumcree Church became known as the Hill.

During the afternoon supporters quickly arrived from Portadown and I said to Olive at 3.00pm, "You must come up to the Hill and see what is happening. You may never see the like again." Little did I know what lay ahead. Among those who came was Joel Patton, who later set up the group "The Spirit of Drumcree", in an attempt to reform the Orange Order and have its link broken with the Ulster Unionist Council. It was not associated with the parish in any way.

The Afternoon   *Olive Pickering*

Supporters came from the surrounding area as well as every part of the province, in a seemingly never ending flow. The road at Drumcree Church as well as the adjacent roads were crammed with people and cars by tea time. The media of the British Isles and parts of Europe began arriving and positioned themselves in the field next to the blockade. The whole of Northern Ireland was mesmerised at what was happening at Drumcree and it all soon became world news.

The Evening

By the time of the normal service at 7.00pm there were many people gathered on the road outside the church and along the churchyard. At the service, attended by 200, people I preached on Psalm 46, highlighting the words "Be still and know that I am God". It was only half an hour before the service that I had decided on that passage for it seemed appropriate in the circumstances.

During the service some trouble broke out at the blockade because of the presence of some outside elements who had arrived and did not understand that a peaceful stand-off was taking place. However, Norman Allen, County Grand Master and Alan Milligan calmed the situation.

After the service was over the crowd grew to about 5,000 people and two short services of prayer were held at the blockade. The first one, which took place at 8.30pm, was led by Cecil Allen Portadown LOL No1 Lay Chaplain, while I led one at 9.00pm along with Rev Percy Patterson, Armagh County Grand Chaplain. Olive spent over an hour organising Percy's visit, assisted by Andrew Robinson.

Everyone received both services with absolute quietness and reverence, the only noise being the buzz of a helicopter overhead.

The Evening   *Alan Lewis/Photopress*

As the evening progressed there was what Graham Montgomery and Richard Whitten described as "a surreal atmosphere – a mixture between a military camp and a scout jamboree."[5]

At about 10.20pm the Rev. Ian Paisley muscled into the fray and addressed the crowd appealing for patience, as efforts were made to obtain permission to parade.

By this time two large crowds of loyalist people had gathered in Portadown, one in Water Street at the lower

5   G. Montgomery & R. Whitten, "The Order on Parade" (GOLI, 1995) p 30

The Protestors *Belfast Telegraph*

end of Garvaghy Road and the other in Charles Street, at Craigwell Avenue. At midnight, as I returned from visiting a sick parishioner, I came into contact with the crowd in Charles Street. One of the crowd said to me, "Tell the people at Drumcree that we will get 10,000 men there on Monday evening." I was not able to drive my car through the large crowd, so a few fellows helped me turn it with certain expletive words to some of the crowd, who were not moving quickly enough for the necessary manoeuvring. One lad, cheered by others, thanked me for coming and said, "You are the only collar who came here today." I returned to Drumcree Church by the Loughgall Road.

All during the night about 800-1,000 determined Orangemen encamped at Drumcree. I will never forget visiting the Parochial Hall that night and as I walked through the Hall I kept tripping over people lying fast asleep on the floor. Others were sleeping in the open air, lying on top of coats and covered with blanketing or sitting on chairs along the roadside, protecting themselves from the chill of the night, under the cover of pages of newspaper. Yet others were awake, some seated, but most were walking about, going to and from the church.

There was a fair amount of chatting and noise all the time. The RUC had forty land rovers at Drumcree and many more such vehicles elsewhere in the town, as well as 900 - 1,000 personnel, who were committed to remain in place until the matter was resolved.

Monday 10th

Just as I was about to go home for some sleep I saw Ian Paisley arriving on the Hill at 2.30am, returning from a visit to Deputy Chief Constable Blair Wallace. I followed Mr Paisley into the Parochial Hall where we met with others in a windowless room at the back of the stage. While Mr Paisley tried his best I did not think he could resolve the matter. However, he always keenly supported my open church door policy. Anyway Paisley asked, "Where is Mr Trimble?" The answer came, "He is asleep in his car." There was silence. Then Paisley spoke again and said, "Well, will someone go and fetch him?" and refused to speak until Trimble arrived. Straightaway one of the brethren scurried off to bring Trimble to the gathering. Quickly Trimble appeared, looking very sleepy and quite dishevelled, as he struggled to straighten his tie. Paisley informed the gathering that there was no change in the situation.

A serious discussion took place and it was affirmed that the stand-off would be continuing. As the meeting was ending some trouble broke out at the blockade. Trimble and Paisley went out immediately to quell the disturbance, by arranging a line of Orangemen between the troublemakers and the RUC, I went home to phone the Northern Ireland Office and if possible to speak with the Secretary of State, Sir Patrick Mayhew (Conservative), but without success.

At daybreak and on into the afternoon, as people kept coming, there was quietness, with the good spirit and humour that there had been the previous day.

As the day progressed I learned that elsewhere supporters of the protest at Drumcree had been angrily making their own protest at RUC stations and by mounting road blocks on the major roads of the country, so bringing much traffic to a standstill. In Belfast and large towns street protests were held, which in some places turned very ugly, with property being attacked and set on fire.

However, later in the day the situation took a new turn, which was to affect the whole province, when it was learned that the port of Larne had been closed and plans were being made to shut down the main electrical generation plant for Northern Ireland at Ballylumford.

RUC in position   *Pacemaker*

At Drumcree people kept coming and going in a 'shift' method of maintaining the protest.

Just after 6.00pm I went up to the Hill and met Jeffrey Donaldson, Assistant Grand Master, who told me about the Mediation Network, headed by Joe Campbell and Brendan McAllister, becoming involved and I encouraged him as he promoted this initiative.

After I had spoken with Mr Donaldson I watched as the already large crowd of Orangemen and supporters began swelling, from 6.30pm onwards.

Lodges with bands and Lambeg drummers from every part of the province, Belfast, Antrim, Down, Fermanagh, Londonderry, Tyrone as well as Armagh, were arriving and parading to the Hill, in what amounted to one long parade that seemed to be never-ending. The cars and buses that ferried them there parked for long distances on

Lambeg Drummers   *Pacemaker*

all the country roads leading to Drumcree, as well as in the surrounding fields.

A large rally was called for 7.30pm in the field behind the church and it commenced at 8.00pm. Olive and I stood at the front of the crowd near the platform to be able to observe the proceedings well. The attendance at the rally was about 10, 000, while the numbers remaining at or near the blockade on the other side of the church from the rally was about 20,000. This was one of the largest gatherings of Orangemen and supporters ever witnessed at Portadown and the largest I had seen since the rally in Omagh in 1951.

The rally was attended by several prominent leaders and addressed by some of them, namely Norman Allen (County Grand Master - Chairman), Harold Gracey, David Trimble, Jeffrey Donaldson, Magnus Bain (Grand Master

Before the Rally   *Olive Pickering*

of Scotland) and Ian Paisley, whose address has become known as his 'do or die' speech, in which he said, "If we don't win this battle, all is lost. It is a matter of life or death. It is a matter of Ulster or the Irish Republic. It is a matter of freedom or slavery."[6]

The following resolution was passed at the rally:

"We, the Orangemen assembled at Drumcree, loyal subjects of Her Majesty Queen Elizabeth, do hereby resolve that we will maintain and defend our civil and religious liberty. We will not accept a ghetto system. As free-born Britons we demand equal treatment with every other British citizen. We repudiate the slander of those who accuse us

6   News Letter 11th July 1995, Irish Times 12th July 1995

The Rally   *Belfast Telegraph*

of triumphal and intimidation in the expression of our cultural and religious identity.

We totally condemn the tyrannous and unnecessary interference with the peaceful procession returning from a Protestant place of worship on the Sabbath day.

We re-assert that the Queen's highway belongs to all law-abiding citizens. No faction, under any pretence whatever, can claim it as their own exclusive territory.

We call upon the police to uphold this fundamental principle. That is their duty to the citizens of this land."

At 9.00pm as the rally was concluding and before Rev. T. R. B. Taylor said a closing prayer, about a dozen unruly youths began to attack the RUC at the blockade. This lasted for about an hour. On hearing this Olive and I decided to go to the rectory and watch from an upstairs window to get a better idea of what was happening. I saw that a group of about 250 people had entered the field beside the blockade and about 24 of them were throwing stones and missiles at the RUC and trying to make their way to the Garvaghy Road. They were soon prevented from doing so by the RUC, who fired rubber bullets.

After intense, but inconclusive, negotiations all day a settlement seemed to be near in the evening at 10.30pm, but it soon faded away because Garvaghy Road was filling with people. Yet at 11.00pm Hester Poyntz phoned me and said, "The parade is going shortly."

I replied, "That cannot be true because I have not been told."

Hester answered, "Well Robert has gone to the town to meet it." As it turned out she was reacting to what she had heard around 10.30pm. To make certain I phoned the RUC about what Hester had told me. The RUC officer said, "There is no word about the parade going." At 1.00am I visited the Orange leaders in the back room of the Parochial Hall and I remarked to them, "There will be no parade tonight," with which they agreed.

So I returned home and went to bed for a badly needed sleep while about 1,000 people were present on the Hill. Later I discovered that the town was full of people who remained all night, expecting the parade at any moment, yet I knew it was not going to happen then, and was free to have a sleep until discussions began again at daybreak.

Tuesday 11th

I rose about 6.30am and drove up the road towards the church where I met Ian Paisley, who was just leaving and he told me that the negotiations of the night had got nowhere, despite talk about a parade at 2.00am.   I continued to the Parochial Hall where I found that a meeting was in progress. A suggested ultimatum that the return parade should begin by 8.00am was rejected as impracticable.   Then I drove David Trimble and Jeffrey Donaldson to the rectory from where Mr Trimble telephoned Sir James Molyneaux, leader of the Ulster Unionist Party.   George Robinson drove Mr Trimble and Mr Donaldson back to the Parochial Hall.

After they left I phoned the Northern Ireland Office with an urgent call for Mr Mayhew to do something about the situation. At 8.15am Assistant Chief Constable Ronnie Flanagan phoned and I told him of the great distress at Drumcree.

I returned to the church and shortly afterwards an agreement was reached. I witnessed the announcement of the agreement by Superintendent T. Houston at the blockade at 8.45am.   The Orangemen were told that a parade was to be permitted, the manner of which was to be that only Portadown District were to parade and without bands. It was also stated that there would be no parade for the eight country lodges on Garvaghy Road on the Twelfth morning, which had been taking place since 1986, after being banned from Obins Street. Shortly afterwards I heard Superintendent Jim Blair repeating this to Harold Gracey twice, but each time Mr Gracey made no response. And the matter was left.

At 9.00am I addressed the Orangemen in a packed Parochial Hall, standing on a wobbly chair. I encouraged them to accept what was agreed and to proceed with the parade.

The agreement was acceptable to the Orangemen, the RUC and the Garvaghy Road residents, who moved to the side of the road.

The parade set off at 10.40am. Mr Paisley and Mr Trimble, who did not belong to Portadown District, did not parade on Garvaghy Road, but did so in the town. They linked hands high in the air at Carleton Street which I think was not necessary and later this image, widely televised, led to an accusation of them being triumphant, which was unfortunate.

Olive and I, exhausted as we were from the activity of the previous three days, were so pleased with the happy and peaceful outcome for everyone. I believe it was a definite answer to prayer. I thought the outcome should be able to serve as an example of how a tense situation could be diffused in an agreeable manner by patient negotiation.

Some time later Superintendent Jim Blair told me that, although there had been much discussion before the agreement,[7] nothing substantial had happened until I had brought Mr Trimble to the rectory.

The remainder of the day

The media coverage of the parade that day highlighted how the Drumcree situation had been resolved, yet hours later uncertainty seemed to have arisen about the Twelfth morning's parade by the eight country lodges. I was very confused by this, as I had heard what Superintendent Blair had informed Harold Gracey about earlier.

Later I heard that there was a meeting that night at Carleton Street Orange Hall to discuss the matter, and an eager reporter phoned me just before midnight to discover the outcome. I told him that it would not be finalised until the next morning, as this is what I had been informed.

Wednesday 12th

The following morning, I went to Corcrain Orange Hall at 7.00am, where the decisive meeting was to be held. While I was not present at the actual meeting the decision was made not to parade along Garvaghy Road but along

---

7   4 See Gordon Lucy, "Stand-off" (USP, 1996), p1-73, R. David Jones and others, "The Orange Citadel" (PCHC, 1996), p62-70, Ruth Dudley Edwards, "The Faithful Tribe" (Harper 1999), p317-332 & 2000 p383-399, Chris Ryder and Vincent Kearney, "Drumcree" (Methuen, 2001& 2002), Dean Godson, "Himself Alone David Trimble" (Harper 2004) p129-145, and Mervyn Jess, "The Orange Order" (O'Brien, 2007) p95-149.

Charles Street to board the buses to the County Armagh demonstration in Loughgall. Since then the Twelfth morning parade has not been held on Garvaghy Road.

At lunch time Olive and I attended the speeches at Loughgall and I was unexpectdly asked to speak from the platform, which I was very pleased to do, even though I felt quite embarrassed because I was casually dressed, while all the other men were wearing their Sunday best suits! I had not expected to be asked to speak, but told them how pleased I was that the impasse had been resolved.

On Thursday 13th July Olive and I left for Dublin for a holiday in the home of Olive's brother Mervyn Young but had to return to Drumcree the next day because Sarah phoned to say that, that morning there had been a firebomb attack on the Parochial Hall and the front doors had been very badly scorched. When I returned I found a Select Vestry meeting already in progress discussing the serious matter and how to prevent possible further attacks. Returning was the right thing to do because my place was to be with my people in time of need.

THE JEWEL PRESENTATION

In September that year a jewel was produced to commemorate the Drumcree stand-off, with the misspelt title "Seige of Drumcree" The first five were presented by Alex Rusk of the Ex-Servicemen's lodge at a ceremony in the Seagoe Hotel on Friday 8th September at lunchtime. I was one of the recipients, along with Harold Gracey, Jeffrey Donaldson, Ian Paisley and David Trimble who later that day was elected leader of the Ulster Unionist Party. It was definitely a memorable day! And so concluded Drumcree One.

Jewel Presentation   *Portadown Times*

Chapter 6
1996 Drumcree Two

THE year began with the explosion of a large bomb at Canary Wharf on 9th February, causing two deaths and much destruction. This was the end of the IRA ceasefire, which had begun on 31st August 1994. At this time Senator George Mitchell was instrumental in the setting up of the Northen Ireland Forum for which elections were held on 14th June. It continued until the 24th April 1998.

JULY

As July approached, Olive and I thought that, as the stand off the previous year 1995 had lasted three days, it would not be allowed to happen again, as it might have worse consequences.

Saturday 6th

However, our worst fears were realised when the RUC announced on Saturday 6th at 12 noon that the parade was not going to be allowed to proceed along the Garvaghy Road after the Church service at 11.30am the following day, because of the fear of disorder.

The Orangemen were very disappointed and there was much anxiety in the whole area and throughout the province. Reporters and cameramen began to arrive in great numbers at Drumcree and in Portadown. And so commenced the giving of many interviews. I appealed for people to remain calm and take events moment by moment, and pray to Almighty God for a peaceful outcome. This meant that again I became extremely active over the days that were to follow.

Sunday 7th - Drumcree Sunday

At 12.30am on Sunday 7th July the RUC under the command of Superintendent C. Robinson, got the army, who had been brought in for backup, to begin erecting a razor wire fence along the field, on the other side of the stream to make sure that nobody reached any further than that point. This was completely unnecessary, as the Orangemen would not attempt to walk along the Garvaghy

The Parade   *Alan Lewis/Photopress*

Road, unless by lawful authority. The fence seemed to be saying that the GRRC were being protected, while LOL No1 was being faced down.

I rose early that Sunday morning, around 5.30am. The security forces were present in large numbers at Drumcree and elsewhere in Portadown. As the morning hours passed there was a great increase in the presence of the media and by 9.00am people began to arrive in the area.

At 10.00am, after Harold Gracey had said, "Drumcree is our Alamo", the parade set off from Carleton Street Orange Hall, Portadown, with all the Officers and David Trimble. It arrived at the church just before 11.30am. As the service commenced there was a great atmosphere of calmness. The large congregation in the church, the Parochial Hall and outside, which altogether numbered

1,300, was very patient, wondering what was going to happen after the service.

However there was a marvellous sense of the presence of Almighty God. I preached on Psalm 4:1 "Answer when I pray God my defender .... Be kind to me now and hear my prayer". Wilson and Wendy Sharpe sang a duet entitled "Who can ever say they understand?". George Robinson, Lay Chaplain Portadown District, read the Old Testament Lesson from Isaiah, Chapter 12 and Robert Wallace, Portadown District Secretary, read the New Testament Lesson from St John, Chapter 14.

After the service the parade formed up and led by Harold Gracey, proceeded to the bridge beyond the church and found the RUC had blocked it with a number of landrovers, police officers and soldiers. The Orange District officers made a formal complaint to the RUC and returned to the top of the Hill.

Then as happened in 1995, another stand–off began. Its nerve centre was set within the Parochial Hall and the Orangemen declared that they were prepared to remain at Drumcree for as long as it took. Just after 2.00pm Rev. Martin Smyth, the Grand Master of Ireland arrived and addressed the crowd and told the people, "Contain yourselves and abide by what your marshals say". In "The Scotsman" he said, "The majority community in Ulster is saying, enough is enough".[1]

During the afternoon crowds of people began arriving from Portadown and the whole province. The roads soon

1   Scotsman, 8 July 1996

became jammed with people and cars. The fields in the area quickly began to be used as car parks. Food began to be served by the wives of the Orangemen, in the Parochial Hall. Mobile food canteens began to arrive. However, all was quiet except for one brief incident involving the waving of a flag. Prayer meetings were held, organised by Rev. Duane Russell, Portadown District Chaplain.

The evening service was held in the church at 7.00pm with about 200 in attendance, and I preached on the verse "They who wait upon the Lord shall renew their strength" from Isaiah Chapter 41:31, which was well received and appeared to have the reassuring effect that God was supreme. Wilson and Wendy Sharpe again sang the duet that they had sung at the morning service.

As the evening continued the number of people present had greatly increased to a very large crowd of about 4,000, with many bands. At the blockade they stood and watched with amazement as they chatted to each other and calmness prevailed. Joyce Gillespie commented to Boris Johnston, whom she met on the Hill, "This is better than any holiday".[2]

However, as nightfall approached, resentment began to build up throughout the province and the RUC became "stretched" because of a great number of road blocks that had been mounted. As the night wore on, unruly elements became active at Drumcree and in other places in the province. This was the beginning of massive protests and many ugly and violent activities, including the burning

2   Daily Telegraph, 10 July 1996

Night time   *Alan Lewis/Photopress*

and destruction of property. At this time, sadly, Michael
McGoldrick, a taxi driver, was murdered near Lurgan.
Along with the Orange Order I strongly condemned the

deteriorating situation and appealed for calm. Firmly I told this element that the Drumcree matter was a dispute between Portadown LOL No1, the GRRC and the RUC and other input was not required.

Monday 8th

At the early hour of 2.30am on Monday 8th I repeated my appeal for calm with a powerful loudspeaker and later discovered that I had wakened my 21 year old daughter Sarah, who was trying to snatch some sleep before an early rise to go to her student holiday job in Moy Park Factory.

Numbers declined during the early hours of the morning, but many did remain on the Hill. As daybreak came and the morning passed there was quietness.

As Monday wore on, the Archbishop of Armagh Most Rev R. H. Eames came and spent a considerable amount of time trying to help find a solution.

During the afternoon at 3.15pm the security forces moved up the Hill a little distance from the blockade and some unrest broke out among the crowd, because it was thought the RUC was preparing to scatter them. I was called to the scene by Trevor McNeice, the sexton, and after making a phone call to the RUC, I was assured that they were simply strengthening their defences by putting large concrete blocks and razor wire on the middle of the road at the bridge, where the road had been blocked by officers. When I conveyed this information by loudspeaker to the crowd, calm was restored both there and on the Brownstown Road where there was unrest because of the RUC moving their position at Drumcree. Eugene Maloney, writing in the Irish Independent, next day said, "Drumcree's Church of Ireland rector spoke over the public address system to assure the Orangemen that the police were simply strengthening their lines, not advancing."[3]

New RUC line   *Belfast Telegraph*

As evening approached, the crowd at Drumcree swelled again to about 4,000. Lodges, accompanied by bands from all over the province, began coming in great numbers, and appeared to be never ending. The bands, along with the sound of the playing of Lambeg drums, created a lively atmosphere. Late in the evening there were spasmodic outbursts from some unruly youths and there was trouble elsewhere.

3   Irish Independent, 9 July 1996 p6

Strengthened line   *Belfast Telegraph*

Tuesday 9th

At 4.30am I rose, visited the Hill and later toured the town at 6.00am to see for myself the extent of the ugly destruction of the previous night, finding some burnt-out vehicles and road blocks still in place. Because of the worsening situation, the Prime Minister, John Major, ordered the deployment of 1,000 extra troops to the province after he had a meeting with David Trimble, Ian Paisley, Robert McCartney and Martin Smyth.

During the day it was quiet. The Archbishop came in the afternoon to visit the Hill. He also spoke to journalists and underlined both the right to parade and the right to protest.

The crowds, which had been arriving all afternoon, increased in the evening as in previous evenings. As the evening wore on with people and vehicles everywhere and bands playing all the time, Olive began to feel light-headed as a result of all the pressure upon her and had to stay away from the crowds for the remainder of the evening.

Lodges Parade to Blockade   *Belfast Telegraph*

Wednesday 10th

I made an attempt to retire early for some much needed sleep, but I was unable to do so because at 12.50am I was asked to arrange for a family to be moved, because of intimidation, and that occupied me until 3.00am. Also between 1.00am and 2.00am I had to attend to an electricity failure at the church, as the NIE engineers would not go to the Hill without my protection! Eventually at 4.30am I got to bed, but had to rise at 6.30am.

The Digger   *Olive Pickering*

By lunchtime I was completely exhausted. Tension and anxiety had built up inside me, as a result of not having had any sleep for the twenty-four hour period from Tuesday morning until Wednesday morning. So I retired to bed at 1.45pm until I was awakened at 5.00pm to be told of a sinister looking mechanical digger with armour plating parked on the Hill, for what purpose I still do not know. With the help of David Trimble, I made sure that the digger was moved to a field to remain there. Then I was alerted about a slurry tanker at the Parochial Hall, but after enquiry, it was explained that the septic tank at the Hall had overflowed and needed to be pumped clear into the slurry tanker. Foolishly many who were antagonistic to Drumcree spread a rumour that oil was being pumped from the church oil tank into the slurry tanker to spread on the RUC.

During the afternoon at the rectory in the room below where I had been sleeping, there was a meeting of politicians including David Trimble, Ian Paisley, Ian Paisley Jnr, Ken Maginnis and Jeffrey Donaldson. Afterwards, David Trimble went to consult with the Archbishop.

As the evening progressed and crowds again began to build up at Drumcree, there were continuous discussions and a number of draft documents were drawn up to seek a resolution. I heard later that David Trimble met Billy Wright, whom I never met, at the Parochial Hall in an attempt to keep him calm.

Thursday 11th

I met with Ian Paisley and other politicians in the Parochial Hall at 2.00am and was brought up to date. I returned at 7.00am to be told that Paisley had left around 3.00am, because of a disagreement about a proposed parade on St Patrick's Day, without having accomplished anything at Drumcree. This turned out to be the end of his involvement in the matter. It seemed that the chances of agreement were lessening. There was also much confusion. Shortly after the News Letter went to print and distribution began, the presses were stopped to change the front page story from "Marchers ready to hit road today" to "For God's sake let them walk".

However at 11.00am I noticed that the RUC land rovers at Drumcree were being turned to face Garvaghy Road. Then after midday events began to move very quickly because at that time, Orange Order leaders including John McCrea, Denis Watson and Stephen McLoughlin, along with politicians David Trimble and RUC ACC Ronnie Flannagan, who became Chief Constable in August 1996, gathered at the rectory for a crucial meeting.

At the same time, unknown to me, a meeting was being held at the Carpet Mills Factory, Portadown, between Archbishop R. Eames, Archbishop C. Daly, Very Rev. D. Allen and Rev. K. Best, the church leaders of the main denominations in Ireland. Those meeting in the factory were unaware of the meeting in the rectory.

When the meeting at the rectory concluded around 12.20pm; I was told by those present that there was going to be a reversal of the decision of Sunday morning and that RUC Chief Constable Sir Hugh Annesley was going to allow the parade to proceed along the Garvaghy Road, leaving the Hill at 12.45pm with one band, Star of David, but no music to be played. This was because of the fear of widespread violence and death if the situation was not resolved by that night, the 11th night.

Immediately I telephoned the Church of Ireland Press Officer, Mrs Elizabeth Gibson-Harries, who had been very helpful to me throughout the past days, in my relations with the media. I was unaware that she was at the Carpet Mills. Immediately she informed the Archbishop and other church leaders, of the decision. Mrs Harries told me they were taken completely by surprise and were stunned by the announcement, which shows me clearly that the Archbishop and the other church leaders had in no way involved themselves in any suggested plot to engage the GRRC in conversation, while plans were made for the parade to proceed. Olive and I hurried to the Hill to witness the departure of the parade. As the parade proceeded along Garvaghy Road it was accompanied by riot police and soldiers.

Looking back I am afraid that I may have made a few mistakes. Probably I should have made contact with the Archbishop to tell him that a meeting to conclude the matter had commenced at my rectory. I had made no contact as I had been waiting for a phone call from him about progress on the whole matter. Not being as close to him as I was later and perhaps a little shy of the Archbishop, feeling that he would be saying, "Don't call me, I will call you", I refrained from making contact.

However I believe, it is true that the Archbishop also made a few mistakes and actually in "Nobody's Fool, The Life of Archbishop, Robin Eames",[4] by Alf McCreary, he acknowledges this. If he had been in more contact with me during 1996, especially during the morning of the Carpet Mills meeting, then I would have told him about the meeting at my rectory. This would have meant that the meeting at the Carpet Mills would have been terminated and a lot of face could have been saved for him

4   Alf McCreary, 'Nobodys Fool' The Life of Archbishop Eames (Hodder 2004) p214

and the others at the meeting. Anyway I am pleased to say that the Archbishop and the other church leaders are to be exhonerated from any blame of collusion.

The parade took place as arranged to the relief of everyone.

For a number of days afterwards, Olive and I continued to be very tense and found it extremely difficult to rest after the events that had taken place, and to settle back to any kind of normal living.

As a sequel to these events, because of an objection to my membership of the Board of Governors of Ballyoran Primary Controlled School, I was prevailed upon to resign from the Board of Governors in September 1996. I did so as I did not wish to cause the school any annoyance or bad publicity, but with regret, as I enjoyed my role in this unique school in the area.

Chapter 7

1997 Drumcree Three

INDEPENDENT REVIEW

AFTER the parade in 1996 and all the events that occurred, the government, with Sir Patrick Mayhew, Secretary of State for Northern Ireland, set up an Independent Review with Dr. Peter North (Chairman), Very Rev. John Dunlop and Rev. Oliver Crilly P.P. in August of that year, and it presented its report on Thursday 30 January 1997.

The Report recommended the setting up of the Parades Commission and the government made appointments to this on 26th March 1997, with Alistair

Graham as Chairman, and members as follows – David Hewitt, Berna McIvor, Roy Magee and Francis Guckian. The Commission at the time had only an advisory role. Shortly after the formation of the Commission, the members drove to my rectory in great style in a new people carrier. I had a long conversation with them explaining the background to the situation, which was followed up by continual discussions with them, as a way forward was sought.

A General Election was held on 1st May after which Mo Mowlam (Labour) was appointed Secretary of State for Northern Ireland. Robert Hamill was murdered on 8th May in Portadown, creating an atmosphere of hostility.

THE GENERAL SYNOD- MAY

Because of the events at Drumcree in 1996 the General Synod of The Church of Ireland in May 1997 proposed to appoint a committee to examine sectarianism.

In a speech at the Synod, I opposed this move as follows:

"The examination of the idea that the Church may be deemed to be accommodating sectarianism at any level, is to create far more problems than it would solve. And certainly the attendance of Orangemen at services in Drumcree must not be included.

The Orangemen attend the service like any other people coming to worship. There must be no doubt about Orangemen attending services.

The stand-off at Drumcree, took place on the public road *after* the service and was *separate* from the service and the Church. The Orangemen held the stand-off because they objected strongly to being prevented from returning to Portadown by the Garvaghy Road, as they had been doing since the beginning of the last century.

The Orangemen, through the stand-off, expressed their objection to, as they see it, their Protestant identity, culture and tradition being curtailed over many years.

What took place outside my church was going to happen somewhere in Northern Ireland and it just happened to take place at Drumcree.

Some unpleasant things occurred for which there is no excuse. But the Orange Order must not be blackened either just because of this. Neither should Drumcree Church be blackened, just because the church building was seen in the background of every television picture and newspaper photograph.

Many of the critics of Drumcree have said many things which sound good from a distance. But I can tell you that it was very different when you live at Drumcree and are present for five days and five nights with thousands of people about and not knowing what the outcome is going to be. Critics need to put themselves in *my* shoes and tell me what *they* would do if they were Rector of Drumcree. Not *one* of my critics has told me.

And do let it be remembered, that it has been said that if the stand off had not been outside *Drumcree Church*, but further along the road, then the influence of the Church for calm would have been absent. It has also been said, "The surprise about Drumcree was not *how bad* it was, but *how mild* it was and *how little* happened afterwards." I believe it was the answer to the prayers of many people.

I do not claim to have the answer to the problem at Drumcree or throughout Northern Ireland. No person but God has the answer to our problems. I feel that the best I can do is to try to make some contribution to bringing calm and peace in my area coming up to the summer and beyond.

I would call upon the Synod members to please pray for me, my wife and family, my parish and Northern Ireland, as we face July.

I oppose this motion because if it is passed, it could open up a whole lot of other problems, as yet unthought-of."

I suggested another motion without "Drumcree" being mentioned in it.

Another speaker from Drumcree, Harry Anderson, Secretary of the Select Vestry, explained how demographic changes in the area contributed to the problem:

"Up to thirty years ago there was no problem; the population was 70% Protestant and 30% Roman Catholic. Now there are sectarian housing estates all around the place. We feel isolated. There is little support within the Church. Our rector took the brunt of everything."

The discussion continued, but the final outcome was that the motion to set up a committee to examine sectarianism was passed.

I was disappointed at this decision, as I believed they were only dealing with a symptom, rather than the whole basic problem at issue.

Subsequently, along with the Select Vestry, I met the committee and a group from the Standing Committee. The Select Vestry explained its position, which was that it supported the right to protest, but that protesting was the role of the Orange Institution, and the parish was not directly involved, but the committee failed to understand this viewpoint.

However I have always had the feeling that many people I met never really understood the issues surrounding Drumcree, remaining so distant from it, and perhaps being swayed by prejudiced viewpoints.

District Council elections were held on 21st May, as a result of which Brendan McKenna was elected to

Craigavon District Council and this gave strength to GRRC.

JUNE

LOL No1 sent an open letter to GRRC on the 4th June, explaining the situation and dealing with misconceptions[1] which had arisen. Civil unrest continued when Constables John Graham and David Johnston were murdered on Church Walk in Lurgan on Monday 16th June, further raising tensions. The government proposed a "gameplan" providing for proximity talks on 27th and 28th June but the talks failed.[2]

JULY

As July 1997 commenced I was wondering what advice the Parades Commission would offer, but they did not say anything.

On Thursday 3rd July in the middle of the events of that week, Olive and I travelled with Sarah to see her degree B.Mus. (Hons.) being conferred by the University of Ulster at Jordanstown at a Graduation Ceremony and had a most enjoyable family day, amid the tensions of the week.

The suggestion by Mr Robert McCartney on Friday 4th July that the right to parade should be declared, but not exercised was rejected by LOL No 1.

1   C. Ryder and V. Kearney, "Drumcree" (Methuen, 2001) p 199
    J. R. Whitten (Ed.) "The Millennium Book" (GOLI, 2000) p 247
2   Ryder and Kearney, p 205 212

Sarah's Graduation

There was much media interest and speculation during the latter part of the first week in July and I gave a number of interviews to media people from near and far, as speculation grew about what might happen during the next few days.

Sunday 6th - Drumcree Sunday

The RUC under the command of ACC T. Craig and Superintendents C. Robinson and M. Bailie, enlisted the army to put fortifications in place. Just after midnight the army began erecting a barbed razor wire fence beside the bridge, "to be ready for all possible eventualities." The work proceeded very slowly with plenty of hammering but with little fence going up, giving the idea that the army did not see any reason for the fence, as the parade was going to be allowed to proceed.

After a short sleep I rose at 5.30 am. I phoned the RUC and enquired about whether the parade would be allowed to proceed along Garvaghy Road. I was told that action had already been taken to allow the parade. By then the RUC in full riot gear, along with the army in an early morning operation just after 3.00am, had moved into the Garvaghy Road and removed protesters, who objected by riotous behaviour. Shortly after 5.00am the RUC and the army began sealing off the fringes of the Garvaghy Road housing estates. By 6.00am 1,000 police and 500 troops were in place.

The NIO said that the decision to allow the parade had been taken: "with regret in the interests of public safety". At 8.30am the new RUC Chief Constable R. Flanagan confirmed that the parade would be allowed to proceed along Garvaghy Road. Mo Mowlam said that the decision was, "dictated by circumstances," which obviously meant that the province was on the brink of eruption.

The parade comprising 1,200 Orangemen, headed by Harold Gracey, the Officers and two bands, the Star of David and Edgarstown Accordian Band arrived at the church at 11.30am for the morning service, where David Trimble was waiting, while a helicopter hovered overhead. The service began with the reading of a statement from the Archbishop in which he called upon the Orangemen "to act with dignity, restraint and honour".

As I began my sermon I said, "Drumcree is a microcosm of Northern Ireland, but I would like to think that Drumcree could be a turning point *for* Northern Ireland, the place where peace could begin and spread from to every part of our country." I preached about St Peter walking on the Lake of Galilee by holding the hand of Jesus. I said, "If people put their faith in the Lord Jesus Christ He would transform their lives and that of the whole country". George Robinson read the New Testament Lesson and the choir sang the piece, "Above the voices of the world around me", while Wendy and Wilson Sharpe sang, "There is no one in the world like Jesus".

All during the service I was very aware that a large number of RUC officers and soldiers in riot gear were holding Garvaghy Road open. There was a cordon of about seventy five jeeps, land rovers and Saracens lining both sides of the road. In this situation my feeling of tension was of course very high and I was aware that every moment I kept the congregation, was a moment longer for the security forces to hold the road.

Immediately after the service, and a speech by Harold Gracey, in contrast to the previous two years, the parade set off. I watched anxiously as the parade left. The men led by Standard Bearer Alec Hyde walked six abreast rather than the usual two abreast to make the parade shorter. The parade was accompanied by Edgarstown Accordian Band with a drummer sounding a single beat. After the parade had passed along Garvaghy Road protests erupted, as they did throughout the province.

In the afternoon the media who were fearful of what might happen, brought all their vehicles and personnel to the Hill for safety and parked outside the church, from where they broadcast all their evening transmissions.

I was very pleased that the Chairman of the Parades Commission had responded to my request to be present at Drumcree to observe the events for himself.

In a surprise move on 11th July, probably in response to Sunday's parade on Garvaghy Road, the Orange Order elsewhere announced that four controversial parades scheduled for the following day, would be voluntarily rerouted. In a series of co-ordinated statements from the local district and county lodges, it was announced that the annual parade in Belfast would not pass through the mainly Catholic section of the Lower Ormeau Road; the parade in Londonderry was switched to Limavady, twenty-five miles away; the parade in Newry was cancelled; and the parade in Armagh City was diverted from the mainly nationalist Shambles district.

My reaction to this was, that I thought that the Orange leaders were trying to demonstrate they were not intransigent, but were trying to be reasonable.

I know that hindsight is a wonderful thing. But in retrospect if LOL No 1, after parading on Garvaghy Road in 1997, could have satisfied themselves that their right to parade was upheld, they could have suspended future parades, without loss of face, until such times as they wanted to parade again, which could have saved all the trouble which ensued from 1998 onwards.

In a surprise announcement the IRA renewed their ceasefire on 20th July, in a statement which was widely welcomed.

In August General John de Chastelain, a Canadian was appointed chairman of the Independent International Commission on Decommissioning to oversee the decommissioning of terrorist weapons.

However, Billy Wright, a local LVF activist, was murdered in prison in December, leading to yet more controversy. Despite speculation that he might be buried in Drumcree where his mother was buried, he was buried at Seagoe Cemetery.

It had been a year of some progress followed by some regression in Northern Ireland as whole, but parish life had continued on an even keel, no matter what had happened.

Chapter 8
1998 Drumcree Four

THE year began badly with the death of my beloved mother on Thursday 15th January. My dear father died on Wednesday 17th July, 1985.

THE SPRING

In the second month there was the dreadful explosion of a massive bomb in the centre of Portadown on 23 February which caused the destruction of much property. Early in the year on 2nd March, the Parades Commission was empowered by the Public Processions Act (NI) to make legal decisions (determinations) about contentious parades. Roy Magee and Berna McIvor left, Roseanne McCormick, Aiden Canavan, Glen Barr and Tommy Cheevers joined, but the later two were soon to be replaced by Billy Martin and Barbara Irwin. From now on it was required that parades are notified on the famous form 11/1, 28 days before hand. I received all the determinations for Drumcree and most of those for the rest of the contentious parades in the province. One July day I received 46 determinations.

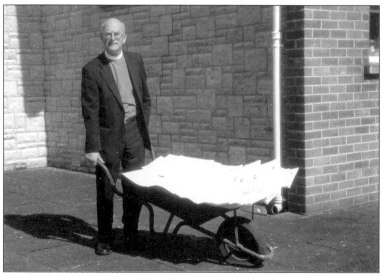

The determinations   *Harry Anderson*

The murder in April of Adrian Lamph brought much tension.

Following months of behind the scene discussions, the Good Friday Agreement (Belfast Agreement) was signed on 10th April 1998, providing for a power sharing

Assembly to be set up for all the political parties in Northern Ireland. This was followed by a referendum on 22nd May in which 71% voted for an Assembly. Elections to the Assembly were held on 25 June. Political progress seemed to be happening at long last, hopefully with the lessons of Drumcree.

JULY

On Monday 29th June the Parades Commission ruled that the parade on Sunday 5th July would *not* be permitted to proceed along the Garvaghy Road so, no change there!

The first meeting of the Northern Ireland Assembly was held on Wednesday 1st July, with David Trimble UUP First Minister Designate and Seamus Mallon SDLP Deputy First Minister Designate. A demand was made for the parade to be allowed, but without success. Denis Watson, Master of Co Armagh LOL said that the Orangemen were "prepared to stay at Drumcree for 365 days."

Mr Tony Blair, Prime Minister, visited Northern Ireland on Friday 3rd to try to dispel growing sectarian tension, after ten Catholic churches had been devastated by fire attacks on Wednesday night. He met with political leaders from all parties and appealed to people to "listen to the voice of reason".

All week I was besieged by the media and I gave about thirty interviews trying to explain the situation and my position in it.

At the end of the week David Trimble phoned me to say that he had decided it was not advisable for him to attend the service on Sunday. This was because of his part in supporting the Good Friday Agreement.

Saturday 4th

Early in the morning of Saturday 4th, I was awaked out of a deep sleep at 2.45am, by the phone ringing at my bedside. It was a call from the RUC under the direction of ACC Tom Craig and Superintendent Charles Robinson saying that the security forces would soon be moving into Drumcree to put fortifications in place, in preparation for Sunday's parade. I nudged Olive and told her what was about to happen. Both of us lay awake and soon I heard the sound of vehicles arriving and on looking out of the bedroom window I saw what appeared to be a never-ending row of lights moving along the Drumcree Road, beyond the church. Other vehicles came past the rectory. Olive said, "I think I'm going to take a heart attack," she was so worried about the situation.

There was much noise, which I discovered by daylight was caused by two large mechanical diggers that were being used to deepen and widen the stream at the bottom of the rectory field. Daylight also showed me that at the bridge beyond the church a razor wire fence was being erected by soldiers on the other side of the stream and a metal barricade 15 feet high, consisting of two large containers, each 25 feet long containing concrete, known as a Crowd Control Obstacle (CCO) was being put in place on the bridge. This operation continued at Drumcree until late in to the afternoon.

Meanwhile the whole of the Garvaghy Road was being sealed off with razor wire and gates which were manned by the RUC. CCTV cameras were put in place, and the whole area was declared a sterile zone, three miles in radius and 3,200 feet high. Again, as in 1996, this exercise was completely unnecessary. It raised tensions, instead of creating calm.

Army Preparations   *Kelvin Boyes/Presseye*

As evening came the whole area was very anxious and everyone was set for another stand-off to begin on Sunday afternoon. I decided that I would help all I could as before, but I would not dash up and down the road endlessly exhausting myself. Actually I had not been feeling in the best of health for the previous six months. I went to bed around midnight each night, though it was very difficult to get to sleep with the constant noise down at the fence, but sleep was a necessity. I rose very early most mornings, 5.00am on Monday, 4.00am on Thursday and 3.00am on Friday. I managed to have a short nap every afternoon, insisted upon by Olive and supervised by her. I was so glad I did make some time for rest, because the whole situation lasted until 20th July.

Sunday 5th - Drumcree Sunday

I rose early on Sunday morning at about 6.00am for I could not sleep any longer, to the annoyance of Olive. I just had to be up making sure I was properly prepared for the service and whatever events the day would bring.

As usual just before 11.30am, the time for the commencement of morning service, the parade from Carleton Street Orange Hall, headed by Harold Gracey and the Officers, arrived at the church. The parade comprised of 5,000 Orangemen, the largest crowd so far to attend since the parade began in 1807. It stretched back from the church away onto the Dungannon Road.

The church and the Parochial Hall where the service was relayed by closed circuit television, by Alex Richardson, were filled to capacity, with Orangemen and parishioners. Thousands of Orangemen crammed the road outside and took part in the service, listening by loudspeakers. As I commenced my sermon I said, "I am sad to see all the razor wire along by the stream, because to me it is a symbol of the division in our country." I preached about the disabled man at the pool in Jerusalem and told how Jesus had healed him and restored him, and how He could rescue and restore all who trust in Him. Billy Grimason sang a solo entitled: 'I Know Who Holds the Future', and George Robinson read the Lesson from St John Chapter 5.

After the service, since the parade was not permitted to proceed, frustrated Orangemen viewed the fortifications and the security forces with disbelief. During the afternoon as the protest got underway, the Orangemen were walking about, chatting and hoping for an early solution. The large crowd remained for most of the day. At 4.30pm some protestors breached the line along by the stream.

Harold Gracey   *David Jones*

When 7.00pm came the normal evening service was held with 200 in attendance and I preached on Psalm 59. This was followed by a prayer meeting in the small hall known as the 'Stables'. Negotiations, were continually being held, trying to find a quick solution. This included what was known as a No 10 Downing Street Conference, which was held by telephone in the rectory study from 10.15pm until 11.15pm, between Mr Tony Blair Prime Minister (PM) and Orange leaders.

I was absolutely mesmerised as I looked out of one of the rectory window at midnight and saw such a great number of people remaining all night in tents, which they had pitched around the rectory field and a field adjoining it. That was their home for the coming days and they were joined by other tent dwellers as the time passed.

THE WEEK BEGINNING MONDAY 6TH

From Monday 6th I was full of anxiety as I did not know what the coming days would bring forth. Conscious of the fact that the Twelfth was a whole week away, I realised that that gave opportunity for trouble to brew before the Twelfth. Every evening crowds of Orangemen with many bands came from all over Northern Ireland and south of the Border, each county coming on a different evening, with two counties on some evenings. These visiting Orangemen, along with the Portadown brethren and crowds of others, men, women and children, came in a seemingly unending flow and crammed the roads. Cars and buses were parked along the roadside for long distances and all the fields in the area, some fields including the rectory field being packed full. There were about 8,000 people on Monday evening.

I phoned Jonathan Powell, the PM's Chief of Staff, at No10 Downing Street at 1.00am on Tuesday 7th to tell him how serious the situation had become and he said he would speak to the PM. 10,000 gathered on Tuesday evening and 16,000 people on Wednesday evening.

Rectory Field   *Olive Pickering*

While there were a few people letting off many fireworks, which brightly lit up the sky, and there being a great amount of noise continually, the first days of the week were fairly peaceful at Drumcree. However, there was dreadful violence in many other parts of the province.

Early on Thursday a delegation arrived from the Church of Ireland Representative Church Body (RCB) and they expressed anxiety about the rectory field being used as a car park. The RCB prepared an Order for the Orange to be expelled from the rectory field and sent it to the Archbishop for me to sign. I refused to sign the Order so it remained in the Archbishop's Office. This showed me the strong authority that lay with a rector. Instead the RCB issued a weak statement.

Later on Thursday, Orange leaders Denis Watson, Stephen McLoughlin, William Bingham and George Patton met Mr Tony Blair in London for talks.

But the situation at Drumcree became serious on Thursday evening 9th, when 20,000 people gathered. At 9.00pm an unruly element infiltrated the crowd, and cut a gap in the razor wire through which many went to the other side. I felt so helpless, as I was unable to exercise any kind of restraint. Some elements were acting in a seemingly mindless manner. Blast bombs were thrown at 11.00pm and a very serious incident occurred around midnight when a blast bomb was thrown, injuring five RUC officers including Chief Inspector John Barr. The RUC, working under their powerful floodlights, responded by firing plastic bullets. It was an absolutely dreadful night.

On Friday 10th, Mr Blair initiated 'Proximity Talks' between the Orange Order and the GRRC. The talks were held on Saturday 11th at Armagh District Council Offices, under the chairmanship of Jonathan Powell, Chief of Staff at No 10, but without success.

By Friday, the numbers were not so large, as each county by then had come to show their support for the protest. Derrycarne LOL No78 attempted to parade to Drumcree from the other side of the church, but were stopped by the RUC and twelve arrests were made.

By Friday night unrest arose with sustained attacks on the RUC by troublemakers and mystery shots were fired from the crowd. It was taken seriously, but later I was told that some ex UDR men standing nearby did not think that they sounded like normal gunfire. Many plastic bullets were fired and a number of people were injured including a woman student who sadly lost an eye.

Every evening, close to the church, there was a carnival air as people met up with old friends and made new ones while partaking of the refreshments that were available in abundance from the tea, soft drinks and burger stalls. I found it very difficult to understand this, while there was so much disorder elsewhere. But then I realised that it was better having that picnic atmosphere than seeing more and more people becoming angry and belligerent. Jack Gilbert, a parishioner, said to me, 'This would be a marvellous experience, if it was not so serious'.

THE WEEK BEGINNING SUNDAY 12TH

Early on Sunday morning 12th, in an outrageous attack on a house in Ballymoney, three brothers called Quinn were cruelly murdered and the Orange at Drumcree were blamed. At his church service in Pomeroy,

Rev. W. Bingham, County Armagh Grand Chaplain, commented that no parade was worth a life. Afterwards he clarified what he had said pointing out that he was not against the Drumcree parade. Thomas Hennessey says, "The motivation was widely regarded *at the time* as resulting from the feverish atmosphere surrounding Drumcree".[1] (My italics)

The normal Sunday services took place at Drumcree with increased attendance. I preached on Isaiah 6:13 about the hope that is always given by God. The funeral of Frank Jones, a parishioner, took place at 2.00pm, as parish life had to continue.

Robert Saulters Grand Master of the Grand Lodge of Ireland arrived at 8.00pm and spoke to the media to say "the protest continues".

The 12th July Demonstration for Co Armagh was held in Lurgan on Monday 13th July, but Portadown District did not attend, preferring to remain at Drumcree.

With the 12th Demonstration on Monday 13th over, on Tuesday 14th Portadown District decided to scale down the protest, but yet maintain it for as long as it took. As fewer people were expected, from then on steps were taken by the Select Vestry to close the gates of the rectory field, as it would no longer be required.

Strangely the Representative Church Body issued a statement on Wednesday morning asking the Orangemen to leave the field, after the gates had already been closed. This was afterwards regretted, because at the time the

---

1   Thomas Hennessey, 'The Northern Ireland Peace Process' (Gill & Macmillan 2000) p197

RCB was unaware that the Northern Ireland Office(NIO) had of course requisitioned the field.

Unfortunately the worst was yet to come on Tuesday around midnight. As I lay in bed I heard a tremendous bang. It turned out to be a lighted gas cylinder that had been exploded at the metal barricade by sinister people. That was the limit, and on Wednesday morning, after I had visited the Hill around 7.00am, the RUC moved on to the Hill at 7.29am. They sealed off the whole area including the rectory field, and made a number of arrests of people who had spend the night in their tents, in a field adjoining the rectory field. The security forces seized the tents and some missiles that were found.

Cleared field   *George Christy*

Until the end of the week the area remained sealed off while the RUC carefully combed all the fields including the rectory field, garden and my potato patch to make sure there were no objects of danger anywhere. This operation brought a few protests because no-one was allowed near the barricade at the bridge during that time.

The army lined Drumcree Road outside the rectory for hours. Some of them slept that night in tents in the rectory field. An army officer told his men not to go outside their tents ill-clad as there was a young girl living in the rectory! They should have known as Sarah had been talking with them earlier in the day.

Sunday 19th - Tuesday 21st

Early on Sunday morning 19th around 5.00am, the army began dismantling and removing their defences in the town near Garvaghy Road. The church services were held at the usual times, again with increased attendance.

At 5.00am on Monday morning 20th, the army began taking away the razor wire fence and the road barricade at the bridge. The area returned to normality. However, the protest was set to continue for however long. The LOL No1 decided to install a large caravan to be manned by Harold Gracey and Bob Guy, as a base near the church, and this was to become an important meeting place over the coming years. Refreshments came to be provided at the "Hillside Café" by May McIldoon and Arlene McKeown assisted by a number of helpers.

At this time LOL No 1 announced that because to their bitter disappointment they were not allowed the July 1998 parade they would be applying for permission to parade every Sunday until it was granted. So began the Sunday protests at the bridge except for the duration of the outbreak of the Foot in Mouth Disease in early 2001.

Orange motif   *LOL No1*

On Tuesday 21st at 9.00am, Olive and I set off for a short holiday to Co Donegal seeking some rest. In August Olive and I visited Olive's sister Ruth and husband Derek in Glasgow. Later, when in Skye on Saturday 15th August, I heard of the Omagh Bomb explosion which resulted in the death of 29 people and the injury of 60. I was absolutely aghast at hearing this dreadful news.

However civil unrest began again towards the autumn and Constable Frank O'Reilly was attacked on 5th September in a confrontation at Corcrain and died on 6th October.

As 1998 continued, many visitors came to the church services, including many lodges, to show their continued support, and I made everyone welcome.

THE CLERGY LETTER

To my surprise, in the middle of the autumn, upon opening my post on 1st October 1998, I found a letter from 160 clergy of the Church of Ireland asking me and my Select Vestry to prevent Orangemen from attending morning service in July. The Clergy went public with this in the Irish News on 5th October. For the rest of that week the press carried the story, and more and more people were wondering how I would react. I summoned a meeting of the Select Vestry on Sunday 11th October, after morning service. The plan agreed was that I would issue a statement to the media the next day. I chose the hour of 7.00pm on Monday 12th October to release my statement. After that the story really took off.

The press release said, "The call to prevent Orangemen attending morning prayer in Drumcree Parish Church in July every year, has been rejected by the rector and his Select Vestry". In the press release I was very definite about my position. "I want to state clearly that I will never deny the right of worship to any person, including any member of the Orange Order". (full text in Appendix B).

The media took up the statement straightway, beginning with BBC Radio Ulster news at 7.00pm and every hour after that until the end of the day. BBC TV (NI) and UTV broadcast the statement, including interviews with me, on their late evening newscasts. Radio and television continued with the story the following morning. David Dunseith, the well known broadcaster, whose programme is listened to by many people, devoted the whole of his programme 'Talkback' to the matter (12noon-1pm BBC daily broadcast). The statement was also carried widely in the press and, pleasingly commented upon positively.

To my great surprise I received about seventy telephone calls of support the next day and many letters for the rest of the week and beyond. I was so grateful for the encouragement I had received from so many people for making my position clear. John Taylor had a letter of support published in the Irish Times, Rev. Donald Collins had a letter in the Church of Ireland Gazette and Rev Bill Hoey wrote in the News Letter.

Many of those who contacted me were very angry, others were most puzzled at even the thought of closing church doors and a large number were actually afraid someone was going to bring considerable pressure on me to close the church. But what came across clearly was that people felt that religious freedom was under threat and that they might be barred from attending church services. I am so glad that my statement was able to bring assurance to those in doubt and distress, that people cannot be prevented from worshipping Almighty God, it is a God given right and a human right, which cannot be denied.

ARMAGH DIOCESAN SYNOD

By Tuesday 20th October 1998, at the Armagh Diocesan Synod, the Archbishop who obviously had come to see that closing the church was not an option, said "It has been suggested by some people that either this service should be banned or members of the Orange Order should not be admitted. This is NOT the way of the Church of Ireland, which is a welcoming Church whose doors are open to all. As Archbishop I uphold that principle."[2]

In a press interview following the morning session of the Synod, I reiterated what I had already said a few days earlier, "The Service at Drumcree goes ahead, as it does every Sunday in our church."[3]

December

Jonathan Powell, the PM's Chief of Staff, held talks at Nutts Corner on 16th December and a few days later, Frank Blair ACAS was asked to help, but it was all to no avail. On Saturday 19th December a special parade of 5,000 Orangemen walked from Portadown to Drumcree to draw extra attention to the stand off. For the occasion a Carol Service and rally were held on the Hill. It was a peaceful end to a turbulent year.

2   Journal of the Synod of Armagh 1998 p11
3   Irish News 21st October 1998

Chapter 9
1999 Drumcree Five

THE SPRING

AS the year began I was hoping for an early resolution, but during the spring and early summer two murders heightened tension, that of Rosemary Nelson on 15th March, and Elizabeth O'Neill on 5th June.

On 4th May David Trimble held a meeting at Craigavon Civic Centre with all the elected representatives in the area, but, unfortunately, it did not achieve anything.

GENERAL SYNOD MAY 1999

As the year 1999 commenced I wondered what the General Synod might say this year about Drumcree. I found out, in due course, when the reports were dropped through my letterbox by the postman one morning at the beginning of May. While I had made my open church door policy clear I was amazed when I discovered that, as a result of the deliberations of the Sectarian Committee, it had been decided to propose three motions to the General Synod on 18th May 1999.[1]

Motion Three, in particular, concerned Drumcree and was the cause of much discontent among many people. The import was to prevent Orangemen from attending morning service at Drumcree in July, even though, as everyone knows, people have the right to worship God. Motion Three stated, "It (The General Synod) calls upon the Rector and Select Vestry of Drumcree to endorse the pledges called for by the Archbishop of Armagh in respect of the conduct of those attending the annual parade by lodges of the Orange Order to Drumcree Parish Church. The pledges are as follows:

"Obedience to the law of the land before and after the service.

Respect for the integrity of the Church of Ireland by word and action and the avoidance of the use of all church property or its environs in any civil protest following the service.

---

1   All three motions are found in the Journal of the General Synod 1999

This Synod further requests that should the Orange Lodges of the Portadown District decline to adhere to the pledges required by the Archbishop of Armagh, the invitation, established by custom, to the lodges to attend morning service be withdrawn by the Rector and Select Vestry of Drumcree."

I spoke against Motion Three saying, "My position is extremely tough. Do not do anything that would make my task more difficult and the whole situation at Drumcree worse. This problem could be in the parish of any Synod member and you would not be able to do other than me, that is to have a pastoral role." I also said, "Nobody can be prevented from attending worship of Almighty God, Orangeman or anyone else."

Immediately after the vote was taken passing the motions I told waiting journalists that I expected the pledges to be fulfilled and that I expected the Orangemen would attend the service in July. This was broadcast live on BBC at 6.30pm and later on other channels. It was also well and widely quoted in the press next day 19th May. Under a front page banner headline in the News Letter, 19 May, "I won't turn anyone away... Rector" it said, quoting me, "I will never prevent anyone going to church to worship Almighty God." The News Letter also quoted my rejection of Motion One which was to prevent the flying of the Union Jack at churches. I had said, "The flying of the Union flag is not unlawful."[2] After all the Union flag is

---

2   Irish Times 19th May 1999

made up of the crosses of Saint Patrick, Saint George and Saint Andrew.

Following the Motion three of The General Synod Portadown District LOL No. 1 received a letter from the Archbishop, dated 17 June, asking for confirmation that the pledges would be complied with, no later than 24th June. The Orange replied saying that they would respond as soon as practicable. So the Archbishop issued a statement in which he said he would wait a further twenty-four hours until midnight 25th June. The Orange response was to reiterate the contents of their letter of 17th May, in which they said that they would always strive to uphold the principles of the pledges. This response was not considered satisfactory.

Meanwhile talks, known as Interpoint Talks, with Frank Blair ACAS on 5th June came to nothing. A proposal was put by Jonathan Powell on 26th June but it did not come to anything because Garvaghy Road Residents Coalition claimed it contained the pre-condition of a parade.[3]

On Sunday morning 27th June I received a phone call asking me to go to the See House in Armagh to collect a letter from the Secretaries of the General Synod and reluctantly I did so. The letter stated, "As a result of the failure of the Orange Lodges of the Portadown District to confirm that they will adhere to the three pledges, and in compliance with the resolution of the General Synod, we now request the Select Vestry of Drumcree Parish to

3   C. Ryder and V. Kearney, "Drumcree" p 301

withdraw the invitation, established by custom, to the Orange Lodges of Portadown District to attend morning service at Drumcree Church this July." From the moment I read the letter I wondered why the words "The Rector," which are in the resolution, were omitted here. I wondered if this was deliberate, as the Secretaries realised it was an impossible request of me as incumbent. I was very displeased at what was being requested in the letter because in no way could I go along with it. Even though the resolution was in the form of a motion I was expected to comply with it and many thought that I would have gone with the motion, but I would never do that.

So at lunchtime, after consulting with the Secretary of the Select Vestry, I made my response through the media and stated clearly that I refused the request and said that anyone who wished to attend the service may do so, members of the Orange Order and anyone else.

The first announcement that I had refused the request, was via Noreen Erskine of BBC. It was made on the Radio Ulster 2.00pm news on the afternoon I had received the letter. The announcement continued to be made throughout the rest of the day. The press carried the announcement the next day.

I was perplexed when I was criticised by the Archbishop of Dublin the Most Rev. Walton Empey for acting against "the will of the church." It was not that I sought a quarrel with the church, far from it, but I was compelled to act according to my conscience. The Church of Ireland Press Officer, Mrs E. Gibson-Harries, made clear afterwards that the authority of the parish lay with the rector and Select Vestry,[4] so the Vestry had rights to reject such a request.

I could not come to terms with the pronouncement of the Archbishop of Dublin, that it could be an option for me to be sacked, as he said on RTE Radio on Monday 28th June at 1.00pm. This was quoted in the Irish Independent and the Irish Times on Tuesday 22nd June. I was never told what the grounds for this opinion were.

For the rest of that week in June, I was aware that I was being closely observed by the Church and the media to hear what more I might say and what I would actually do on the Sunday morning of 4th July.

Barricade   *Olive Pickering*

JULY

The Parades Commission determined against the parade for 4th July.

During that week Dana Scallon of Eurovision Song Contest fame, phoned me asking if I could arrange a meeting for her with Harold Gracey, which I did. The meeting which was held on Wednesday 30th June, went well and Dana said she would sing at a concert in the Orange Hall any time! At the end of the week the now familiar razorwire fence was put in place along the stream and a huge high metal barricade was put in position on the road at the bridge by the Royal Engineers. I observed the protest was also seen as a protest against the Good Friday Agreement. So if a parade was allowed, then opposition at Drumcree to the Agreement would be removed and the Agreement would be strengthened. Confusion arose about a desire for a parade. Some people ended up not knowing whether they did actually want the parade to proceed. This situation remained until the clarification of the St Andrews Agreement. This year also saw at Drumcree and in Northern Ireland the Royal Dragoon Guards, 32 Regiment Royal Artillery, Ist Battalion Cheshire Regiment and Ist Battalion King's Regiment along with the Royal Irish Regiment.[5]

---

5   Other years saw the Scots Guards, the Highlanders and the Argyll and Sutherland Highlanders, The Prince of Wales own Regiment of Yorkshire, The Devonshire and Dorset Regiment, The Parachute Regiment, The Royal Green Jackets, The Royal Anglican Regiment and The Royal Regiment of Fusiliers.

Soaking the ground   *Pacemaker*

Sunday 4th - Drumcree Sunday

When my watch showed 6.15am on Sunday 4th July I rose
to face the day, whatever it held. I visited the church at
7.00 am. At 7.45am I gave an interview on Radio 4
repeating my welcome to all comers. Then I saw water
being poured from a helicopter to dampen the bank of the
stream which had been ploughed by the army but without
much success. After breakfast the next couple of hours
passed quickly until it was time for Olive and me to go to
the service. A large number of Orangemen left Carleton
Street Orange Hall shortly after 10.00am on parade to
Drumcree Parish Church, without the District banner, as
it was still at Drumcree. Instead they carried a banner
with the words, "Our Bannerette is still at Drumcree".

Substitute Bannerette   *Kelvin Boyes/Presseye*

At the service there were about 6,000 Orangemen and other people, including 1,000 people belonging to the Long March, which was formed to draw attention to the plight of the victims of violence over the previous thirty years. They had been walking from Londonderry since the previous Monday. I was absolutely overwhelmed by the enormous crowd of people who came to Drumcree that morning. This was the largest attendance ever recorded at Drumcree. To me this clearly reflected the groundswell of opinion against the General Synod motion. This large number of people was an historic moment for religious freedom. It gave me great pleasure to welcome the Orangemen and everyone else who attended. As I did so I asked myself how anyone could ever refuse these people the right to worship.

It was quite an experience to conduct the service in a packed church and to have it relayed by closed circuit TV to the Parochial Hall, which was also packed with worshippers, and by loudspeakers to the huge crowd of people outside. I felt greatly strengthened by Almighty God as I led the worship and preached the sermon. The Old Testament Lesson was read by George Robinson, while Betty Best sang a solo entitled *God will take care of you*, with Trevor Sharpe playing the organ. The service was most reverent with everyone keenly participating.[6] Patsy McGarry writing in the Irish Times on Monday 15th July said, "At Drumcree yesterday, the Orangemen came. They saw the two Union Jacks flying from the dreary steeple. And they congregated inside once more for morning service. Yesterday at Drumcree it was as if the

Service in progress   *Pacemaker*

6   See Ulster Gazette 8th July 1999

General Synod of the Church of Ireland last May had never happened."

After the service the Officers of Portadown District paraded down the road, passing crowds of people on either side. When they reached the barricade a small door swung open and Superintendent Mervyn Waddell stepped through. He was handed a letter of protest against not being allowed to return to Portadown along Garvaghy Road. When Nigel Dawson asked for the parade to be allowed, Waddell replied, "I am not permitted to do that."[7]

Then a plan that I had conceived, and agreed with the Orange, was put into action. All on the Hill were asked to make their way to the rectory field for a briefing. At that time Olive was already at the rectory assisting Robert

Meeting at Rectory   *Olive Pickering*

7   The Mirror, 5th July 1999

Oliver to get amplification ready for the speeches to be made. I am very glad to say that the crowd responded admirably and went very willingly to the field. No-one knew why the crowd was being moved or what announcement was going to be made, except the District Officers and myself. The media was taken by complete surprise and had no idea what was going to happen next.

As soon as the crowd arrived it was addressed by Harold Gracey, who affirmed that the protest would continue and that it was to be peaceful. He appealed for troublemakers to stay away. The exercise was most successful and prevented a potentially tense situation at the barrier from becoming very dangerous, although LOL No. 1 were very disappointed after all the discussions they had, especially with Tony Blair, that they were not allowed to parade along Garvaghy Road.

Irony   *Olive Pickering*

Unfortunately there was never enough credit given for the success of this exercise towards the peace that followed, except by Mediation Network and Dr. Alan Acheson.[8] I am very grateful for these references. And I could never see that the calm of 1999 came about because of special adherence to the pledges of the General Synod Motion, as was reported to be claimed in Alf McCreary's Nobody's Fool-The Life of Archbishop Robin Eames.[9] Clearly the exercise was successful because of prayer. While protestors continued to be present on the Hill from

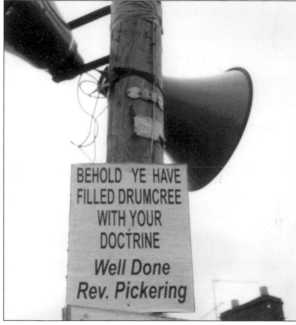

A Tribute   *Olive Pickering*

8   Alan Acheson,"History of the Church of Ireland 1691-2001" p. 277
9   Nobody's Fool p 221

then onwards everything was remarkably calm, thank God. This situation continued throughout the whole week and to 'The Twelfth' and beyond. The fortifications were removed on Wednesday 14th July.

SEPTEMBER-DECEMBER

A series of proximity talks began on 24th September by Adam Ingram and George Howarth, two Ministers of State, but they did not produce any results. The protest against the re-routing was maintained continually on the Hill.

Power was devolved from Westminster to Northern Ireland on 1 December. David Trimble UUP became First Minister and Mark Durkan SDLP Deputy First Minister.

Greeting Peter Mandleson
Paul Faith/PA

A few days before Christmas Mr Peter Mandleson (Labour), Secretary of State for Northern Ireland, visited Drumcree and met the leaders of Portadown District LOL. The meeting took place in the small 'Orange' caravan on the Hill and I was privileged to be present. The meeting was private and was very useful as it provided me with access to Mr Mandleson for the rest of his time as Secretary of State.

Chapter 10
2000 Drumcree Six

JANUARY

As the year 2000 began, with all the talk of entering the new century, I wondered what the year would bring forth in relation to the problems at Drumcree. From that time occasional brief spasmodic protests were held throughout the area by "flying pickets."

EARLY SPRINGTIME

For the next three years from 16th February the following were appointed to the Parades Commission – Tony

Holland (Chairman), John Cousins, Roy Magee, Billy Martin, Peter Osborne, John Pringle and Peter Quinn.

At that time I was pleased to meet Mr Brian Currin, a South African human rights lawyer who had been appointed by Mr Peter Mandelson to mediate in the dispute, in the early springtime. Soon he was very active in talking with LOL No 1, GRRC and the Parades Commission. I had great hopes for his involvement, as I knew he was a man of great integrity and foresight.

From 11th February until 29th May the Northern Ireland Assembly was suspended. Northern Ireland was again in a state of limbo and I wondered if this would make any difference to our situation at Drumcree.

JULY

Sunday 2nd

As the time wore close to July, the Orange was advised to have their parade to morning service on Sunday 2nd, a week before their traditional parade. The idea was that it might be easier for a parade to be allowed along Garvaghy Road on Sunday 2nd than on Sunday 9th. However the Parades Commission refused permission for the parade. Anyway on Sunday 2nd a large number of Orangemen from other Co. Armagh districts, other than Portadown, paraded and joined Portadown at Drumcree - Portadown were already at Drumcree, not having officially left since July 1998! They all attended morning service without wearing collarettes at the service.

After the service, under the command of ACC S. White the road was blocked at the bridge simply with RUC and army vehicles. Harold Gracey spoke at the bridge and called for country wide protests to be held every day that week.

The advice about holding the earlier parade proved to be bad advice because unruly elements came during the following days leading up to Sunday 9th.

The afternoon of the 2nd was quiet. Evening service took place at 7.00pm followed by a special prayer meeting in the church from 8.00pm-9.00pm. Later, a large crowd gathered on the Hill as in previous years. As darkness began to fall some trouble broke out and I saw that an army vehicle had been set alight. I feared for the coming days, so I decided to try and encourage people to move from the bridge, lest anyone would get hurt.

Monday 3rd

At 12.20am in an effort to make sure that disorder did not break out an RUC riot squad cleared the road of all people from the bridge to beyond the Parochial Hall. At that time Olive and I were at the Parochial Hall so we were trapped[1] inside, until 1.00am, as a tense stand-off took place between the RUC and the crowd. After 1.00am tension eased, but some of the crowd remained until 2.00am. Then the RUC asked if I could bring the impasse to an end, which I am pleased I was able to do by asking the

1   The Rector, the Rev John Pickering was trapped in the Church Hall" Portadown Times 7 July 2000

remaining people to leave, as they had been there quite a long time. I phoned the RUC at 3.00am, and I was assured all was quiet. At 3.16am I climbed into bed.

Later in the day, at 12 noon, the Parades Commission issued its determination for the parade on Sunday 9th, once again preventing the return via the Garvaghy Road. However, a scenario called a "road map" was set out, by which a parade could take place in three to eight months, time. It stated:

"For this to happen it would be necessary for the Portadown District and the Orange Order more generally to comply with the terms of the Commission's determination. Introduce an immediate moratorium on Drumcree-related protest parades and demonstrations. Avoid any actions that could reasonably be perceived as an incitement to break the law or intentionally designed to raise intercommunal tension. Engage along with representatives of the Garvaghy Road residents, in the Currin initiative in any civic forum that may be established and undertake that following any parade the protest vigil at Drumcree would not resume"
(Parades Commission 3 July 2000)

In the evening about 7.30pm I saw the UFF appearing on the Hill with Johnny Adair UDA/UFF and I spoke briefly to some of them, who assured me they would not stay long. They left about 9.30pm. A fire was lit at the barricade after 10.00pm and some bad disturbances broke out, so at 11.00pm the RUC cleared the area so that disorder would be prevented. Everything settled down very quickly, and Olive and I finally went home, satisfied that all was quiet.

Tuesday 4th

On Tuesday morning, because of my experience of the disturbance the previous evening I decided to issue a statement to the media appealing to women and children not to remain on the Hill if they saw any disturbance arising. The RUC Chief Constable Sir Ronnie Flanagan said in a TV interview that I had not said enough.[2] Olive was distressed and wrote to him saying that I was doing my best in extremely difficult circumstances and she later received a polite, hand written reply.

Later that evening, as tension rose, I observed the use of a water cannon for the first time in Northern Ireland in many years. It was supposed to disperse the crowd at the bridge, but without success, as the crowd enjoyed it and kept returning for more. This was a very anxious time, but around midnight the larger part of the crowd had dispersed, with the help of Paul Berry MLA.

Wednesday 5th

Steps had to be taken to try to prevent further tension so in the morning the high metal barricade (20 feet x 30 feet)

---

1   News Letter 5 July 2000 p 4, Irish Times 7 July p 6, Portadown Times 7 July p 6

Water cannon   *Pacemaker*

of the previous year was erected on the bridge by the army
engineers and this diffused the tension.

Thursday 6th

Harold Gracey and Portadown LOL No 1 presented a
lengthy and detailed submission to the Parades
Commission through their legal advisor Mr Richard
Monteith. Harold's statement read: "I am the District
Master of Portadown District Orange Lodge No 1 and have
been since 1986. I list here a series of meetings and

events in which I, together with the other District Officers from Portadown, have taken part, in an effort to resolve the difficulty in returning from morning worship at Drumcree Parish Church to Carleton Street Orange Hall, via the traditional route of the Garvaghy Road. I refer to a list of meetings between the 6th July 1998 and the 15th July 1999.[3] It concluded with five pledges, as follows -

On behalf of Portadown LOL No1 I would give the following pledges in the event of a parade being permitted By Portadown District LOL No1 from Drumcree Parish Church via the Garvaghy Road to Carleton Street Orange Hall on 9th July 2000:-

(i) To immediately cancel all rallies, protests and parades and other related activities which have been notified or planned. There will be no further protests or associated events concerning the Drumcree issue, as the cause of the protest from July 1998 will have been effectively removed.

(ii) To continue to engage in the premediation process set up by Brian Currin, with a view to moving to full mediation and an attempt to resolve the parades issue for 2001 and all future years.

3   News Letter 7 July 2000, p 8, Irish Times 8 July 2000 p 2

(iii) To continue to publicly urge that all issues surrounding the Drumcree Parades dispute be resolved peacefully and without re-course to violence of any kind.

(iv) To have Portadown LOL No1 Representatives take part in any Civic Forum established assuming that Orange Representatives are invited to attend.

(v) The parade, while it passes from Drumcree Church to Shillingtons Bridge, will be limited to Orangemen from Portadown District LOL No 1. Bands or Orangemen from other areas will not be permitted to take part.

Friday 7th

At 3.00am I was awaked from a deep sleep, to receive a phone call from the RUC informing me that a razor wire fence was going to be stretched across the fields beyond the stream from the bridge to Dungannon Road and Derryanvil Road. So I was required to rise and unlock the rectory field gates to let the army enter, as they were to surround the whole area during the operation.

The News Letter announced later that morning that LOL No1 had offered to engage in talks with GRRC, if a parade could take place ahead of talks. Nothing came from the offer. Later during the morning Harold Gracey, in an interview with Peter Hunt of the BBC, while saying that he was not a violent person remarked, "I am not going to condemn violence because Gerry Adams never did."[4]

The Portadown Times that day quoted David Thompson UU who said, "No individual or group should have to receive permission from another before it can exercise its human rights, its freedom of peaceful assembly and its freedom of expression".

Sunday 9th - Drumcree Sunday

I rose early as in previous years. A very large number of Orangemen paraded from Carlton Street Orange Hall just after 10.00am and joined with Portadown Orangemen at Drumcree to attend morning service. The service was relayed to the Parochial Hall and outside was attended by about 5000 people. I conducted the service, the Lessons were read by George Robinson and Cecil Allen and the soloist was Billy Grimason, who sang, "Have Thine own way Lord."

In my sermon I said, "The barricade in the "valley" of the bridge speaks of diversion, separation, but the church on top of the Hill is a symbol of agreement and hope."

After the service the Orange paraded down to the bridge where crowds of people were waiting. A protest was made against the re-routing, speeches were made and the Orange parade dispersed. There was a heavy shower of rain and a BBC commentator attributed it to the 'divine

4   Irish News 8 July 2000

intervention' I had been talking about earlier in the week but of course I had meant that divine intervention was necessary to resolve the situation at Drumcree.

Many people remained and the crowd grew as the day went on. Evening service took place at 7.00pm, but as all remained calm Olive and I returned to the rectory at 8.00pm. Later in the evening around 11.00pm, because of disturbances at the barricade involving a fire I saw a large contingent of soldiers being flown in by helicopter, in quick succession. Then a large squad of RUC arrived in a convoy of vehicles, with bright blue flashing lights. All this heavy deployment of security forces immediately began moving the crowd from the Hill, across to the rectory field and onto Drumcree Road near the rectory gates. There it halted and a nasty stand-off began at 11.30pm, because some of the crowd refused to disperse. Olive and I remained in the rectory with all the lights switched off, peeping out apprehensively between the curtains. Any observer would have said that he saw two very nervous people. Eventually about 2.00am I ventured out towards the middle of the lawn to watch from there, but was soon called back by my anxious wife. Then I offered help to the RUC but it was not required, as the crowd had begun to disperse.

The Rest of the Week

There were large numbers of people at Drumcree until Wednesday which was the Twelfth but it was generally quiet.

However elsewhere in the county serious unrest occurred with attacks upon the police particularly at Corcrain and West Street Portadown. When Friday morning, the 14th, came the army removed fortifications. Work on removing razor wire commenced at 3.00am and the barricade was removed from the bridge at 9.00am.

The protest continued however, although on a smaller scale than previous years, with the Orange remaining determined to maintain their stand-off on the Hill.

SEPTEMBER

After the dreadful events of July the Archbishop suggested that the Select Vestry should issue a statement, disassociating the church from the violence.

At the first meeting of the Select Vestry of Drumcree Parish since the July period held on Wednesday 13th September, the Select Vestry and I issued the following statement:

"We are aware of the perceptions abroad that the Rector and Select Vestry of Drumcree Parish carry moral responsibility in relation to events caused by unruly elements who exploited a legitimate peaceful protest, following Morning Prayer attended by members of Portadown LOL No 1. We feel we have a duty to the parishioners of this church and to the community at large to make our position clear.

We totally disassociate the parish from the violent scenes which have been orchestrated by certain so-called supporters of the legitimate protest of the Order, the violence witnessed across the province in July and the suffering caused to so many innocent people. We disassociate the parish from all such activity which has turned a peaceful protest at the denial of human rights into a period of unlawfulness.

We support all efforts to reach a solution to the current impasse, but we must make it clear that we wish to continue to maintain a normal parish life through regular worship of Almighty God.

We pray and ask others to pray that a resolution will soon emerge for this ongoing situation.

We appreciate the support, concern and effort of our Archbishop and many other to reach a solution."

CONCLUDING MONTHS

During the months of November and December efforts were made by the Archbishop and Brian Currin to find a solution to the parading problem. The matter was made worse by the Dunloy Judgement in which the High Court refused leave for a judicial review of the Parades Commission ban on a parade in Dunloy on 29th October 2000 saying that they were satisfied the restrictions were necessary for the prevention of disorder. It is a pity an application was made for the review because the result was it set a precedent, which meant that no other lodges making application could expect a judgement in their favour.

I was present at a meeting held in late November where it was decided that a proposition would be communicated to GRRC involving proximity talks to be followed by a parade. This proposal was set out in a letter to the Parades Commission from LOL No1 sent by Richard Monteith via Brian Currin, for a parade on 10th December 2000 or 17th December 2000. The letter was not acted upon by the Parades Commission, a strange and disappointing decision.

To facilitate progress I suggested to the Parades Commission that it would make it easier for the LOL 1 to speak to them if they stated that they would not make it obligatory for LOL 1 to speak face to face with GRRC. Unfortunately nothing materialised from my suggestion at that time. A request was made by LOL 1 to GRRC, again via Currin in December asking them for their reasons for objecting to the parade. No reasons were given.

Nevertheless, at the end of December there was actually a feeling of hope that an agreement might be reached and a parade take place in the foreseeable future.

Chapter 11
2001 Drumcree Seven

JANUARY – JUNE

JANUARY began with Peter Mandelson resigning as Secretary of State for Northern Ireland on 24th and being replaced by John Reid (Labour). The resignation came about because of a question over a passport application for a wealthy businessman, some time before Mandelson became Secretary of State. Personally, I found that Peter Mandelson was a man with whom I could work and I appreciated the discussions I had with him.

At a special meeting of the Grand Lodge of Ireland held on 3rd February, to discuss a "Parades Policy Document", one hundred and fifty copies of a 2,700 word report from Brian Currin was produced, but it was not distributed, even though Currin felt it was very important. In his written representation Currin said, "The fairest and most effective way of judging the integrity of the Parades Commission would be to test its Guidelines and determinations against the application of European Human Rights Law. It is for that reason that I decided to research European Jurisprudence on the relevant points and to that end have identified and analysed all the relevant cases over the past twenty years. The stark reality is that the right of assembly, which covers public processions, is not enforceable in an environment where procession will inevitably result in serious public disorder" (1st February 2001).

Currin emphasised this stark reality to me in a telephone call from South Africa in mid February. I believe that this serious reality amounted to what is called a "rioter's charter", that is, it appears the threat of violence is enough to stop a parade and showed the need for the Orange Order to engage pro actively with the Parades Commission.

A proposition was made in February by the GRRC offering a parade outward and inward via Charles Street, in perpetuity, on the understanding that the Garvaghy Road would be forfeited forever. This was rejected by LOL No 1.

As the springtime came the Parades Commission kept drawing back from solving the problem, saying that it was up to Brian Currin as he was "the only show in town". But LOL No1 had broken contact with Currin at this time. However in late spring they began to engage again with Currin and so with GRRC, but to no avail. At this point I was reaching despair, because I saw that nothing was happening. So I suggested to the Archbishop, Robin Eames, that I believed he was the person who could kick-start the process and get some action going, for the good of the whole of Portadown. And this he did.

After this a series of meetings began between LOL No1 members H. Gracey, D, Burrows, S. Thompson, R Monteith, and D. Watson and J. Campbell and the Archbishop, at which I was present, some of them continuing until after midnight, but unfortunately no progress was being made, even though there was communication with the Parades Commission, Brian Currin and John Reid.

A General Election was held on 7th June in which the UUP lost three of its nine seats because of anti-Agreement feeling.

In mid June as Drumcree Seven was looming I arranged with the Archbishop that because an impasse had again developed, to seek a meeting with the Parades Commission, for making progress for the good of everyone in Portadown.

The Archbishop and I went to the Parades Commission on Friday 29th June 2001 at 12 noon, with a degree of optimism, because the Parades Commission appeared to have become more realistic about parading, in their determination for the weekly parade on Sunday 1st July 2001. In that determination the Parades Commission said that any attempts at engagement by LOL No1 were seen as a movement in the process.

"As stated in paragraph 4.4 of the guidelines, the Commission also takes into account any communications between parade organisers and the local community or the absence thereof. Further, the commission will assess the measures, if any offered or taken by parade organisers to address genuinely held relevant concerns of members of the local community.

As indicated at page 15 of its second Annual Report, the Commission (while avoiding an excessively prescriptive approach) considers the essence of engagement to be attempts at genuine communication (whether direct or indirect) between protagonists to a particular parading dispute."

I suggested that the documents that had been passing between LOL No1 and GRRC over the previous months surely ought to amount to some attempts at engagement. But the Parades Commission would not accept these documents as sufficient engagement.

The Archbishop made a good case for a forum to be established to address all the problems of Portadown, but the Parades Commissions thought the idea of a forum may be regarded as a way of procuring a parade. I thought the setting up of a forum had great potential for Portadown.

Unfortunately the visit by the Archbishop and I did not accomplish anything, for the immediate future anyway.

I returned home very disappointed, feeling that the Parades Commission did not have the will to solve the parading problem. I came to the conclusion that the Parades Commission, which had been set up to solve the parading issue was failing miserably and indeed made the matter much worse. It was not that I was blaming any individual members of the Parades Commission, but rather finding fault with the whole idea of the Parades Commission. My feeling was that the Parades Commission should be replaced as soon as possible, and many people agreed with me.

JULY

And so on Monday 2nd July 2001 at 6.00pm the Parades Commission issued its determination for Sunday 8th July 2001, and as was expected, it banned the parade from Garvaghy Road yet again.

However, a review was asked for by certain Unionist Councillors from Craigavon District Council: Jonathan Bell, David Simpson, Arnold Hatch and David Jones.

They met the Parades Commission on Tuesday 3rd July. While they were members of the Orange Order, they went to the Parades Commission as Councillors. David Jones said that day in "Rite and Reason" in the Irish Times, "The Orange delegation has consistently asked, during each process, what needed to be done to make the parade more acceptable to the Garvaghy residents. No answer has been forthcoming. The residents' only interest was in discussing issues unrelated to the parade and about which the Orange Order can do nothing"

A plea to protect the tourist industry was made to the Parades Commission on Thursday 5th July 2001 at 9.00am by Sir Reg Empey, Minister of Tourism and Trade along with Michael McGimpsey and David McNarry.

At 11.30am I received a phone call from William Bingham, County Chaplain telling me that at the end of Sir Reg's visit, the LOL would be making a 20 page written submission to the Parades Commission. This submission was delivered to the Parades Commission at 11.34am. Unfortunately it was rejected in the surprisingly short time of an hour, or maybe less. That afternoon at 3.00pm the Parades Commission issued a review in which they upheld their determination of 2nd July for Sunday 8th July.

I was again so disappointed that the Parades Commission was not grappling with the issue. It is interesting that at that time the GRRC set out for the first time, their objections to the parade, which they enumerate as ten.

1. The march was perceived as being of a triumphalist nature;

2. There was considerable fear about individual safety as well as the effect the parade would have on the area;

3. The lack of direct engagement implied a clear lack of respect for the Garvaghy Road Residents;

4. There was concern that the Orange Order, despite evidence being available, not disciplined members who had engaged in disturbances, intimidatory behaviour or other actions against Catholics;

5. There was concern about ongoing loyalist anti-social activity in the area around Corcrain Orange Hall;

6. There was concern about ongoing loyalist anti-social acitivity in the area around the Garvaghy Road area;

7. There was no confidence that the leadership of the District could control any parade, given that they had failed to prevent protests degenerating into disorder and failed to control other parades in the past;

8. There was concern about behaviour at this particular church parade over the past 30 years or more;

9. There had been enormous damage to community relations in Portadown as a result of the parade;

10. There would be a strong feeling of humiliation on the part of nationalists if the parade were to go down the road without agreement.

Saturday 7th

When Saturday morning came, very early about 1.00am I looked out of the study window of the rectory and saw the lights of a long vehicle, which was being driven slowly past the rectory, in the direction of the church. Just beyond the rectory gates the vehicle came to a halt. Straining my eyes I peered through the Venetian blinds, to see what was happening. I dashed down the avenue and saw the vehicle was an army one with ploughs on board which were to be used to plough a section of the rectory field at the stream, which again was to be the dividing line between the 'Orange' side and the 'army' side.

The army engineers had just, with great difficulty, manoeuvred their tractors through the narrow gate of the small field. I called to the men, "Hey squaddies, you are in the wrong field, you are not supposed to go in there because the gate is too narrow."

"But," they replied, "the gate on the big field is narrow also. "No," I said, "there are double gates there with a bar in the middle which can be removed to allow large vehicles to enter easily!" However, they missed the wide gate, but eventually they reached the bottom of the big field, through the small field and began to plough about 1.30am. I went to bed.

At 3.15am, unable to sleep, I looked out of my bedroom window, but there did not seem to have been much progress made with the ploughing. I climbed back into bed until 6.30am. Upon rising and looking out of the window I saw that the ploughing was progressing very slowly indeed, with only a couple of furrows ploughed. What happened was that the previous day, Harry Eldon, the tenant of the land, had mowed all the weeds in that area, some being five feet tall! He happened to leave all the cuttings in the ground and they got entangled in the plough, so in the dark the ploughmen could not see what they there doing! I observed that on the other side of the stream the army had commenced to erect the usual razor wire fence. I saw that work had begun to put the familiar barricade in place at the bridge.

By mid morning the usual round of media interviews had begun, which were now characteristic of the Saturday before the Orange Service Sunday. The interviews were with BBC (NI and World Radio), Sky, RTE, APTN, ITN, C4, TV3, Spanish TV, Downtown, CNN, ITV and TG4. It

Ploughed field at stream   *Olive Pickering*

was 3.30pm before the interviews were finished. I worked till late in the evening making final preparations for the service the next day.

Sunday 8th - Drumcree Sunday

At a quarter to six in the morning I rose to face whatever the day sent. I did a live interview with BBC 24 at 7.15am. After a quick breakfast at 7.30am I put the finishing touches to my sermon, which would be delivered in a few hours time.

I set off for church in good time for the service. To facilitate the overflow of worshippers a closed circuit TV system had been put in the Parochial Hall.

A TV company positioned a high hoist outside the church gate to get pictures from the church side. I was glad of this venture, as it kept the church from being in the background of every picture that was broadcast that morning

At 11.15am the parade of Orangemen including for the first time Orangewoman began arriving at the church from Carleton Street Orange Hall. There were about 2000 this year, not as many as usual. The reduction in numbers was not relevant as far as the protest was concerned because the numbers varied from year to year. The manner of the protest had also varied over the years.

At the service Betty Best sang a solo entitled "In times like these you need a Saviour", while Cecil Allen read the Old Testament Lesson and George Robinson read the New Testament Lesson. I preached about the demon possessed man of Gadara in St Mark, Chapter 5, to show that no matter how difficult a situation may be, there can be healing.

After the service Harold Gracey and the Officers paraded to the barricade and made the usual protest to the RUC under the direction of Superintendent C. Donnan and Superintendent H. Cully. I observed this action from the graveyard and I must say it was quite amusing to see a section of the barricade, which looked like a door, suddenly being swung open and a RUC officer coming out to receive the protest, flanked by a number of police bodyguards in full protective clothing. After the policeman returned and the 'door' was closed, soldiers welded it secure.

Then speeches were made by some of the Orange Officers. They were prefaced by a Bible reading and prayer by Cecil Allen, District Chaplain. The speeches were made by David Burrows, Deputy Master of Portadown District LOL, Denis Watson, Grand Master of Co Armagh LOL, Robert Saulters, Grand Master of the Grand Lodge of Ireland and Harold Gracey. As Harold Gracey concluded his speech he said, "Keep calm and keep the protest peaceful for the sake of the Reverend Pickering and the Church." Then he dismissed the parade and said, "Nevertheless the protest will continue until such times as the brethren of Portadown District LOL No 1 are allowed to parade from the church along Garvaghy Road back to the Orange Hall in Carleton Street."

The Week Following

From Sunday afternoon, I am pleased to say that all was quiet except for a few minor incidents. A few bales of hay which had been brought by several 'burly' boys on Monday 9th, were set alight at the barricade. They were still smouldering the next day. But after I summoned the fire brigade the fire was soon extinguished, and the debris was removed when Sydney Anderson summoned a Borough Council cleansing lorry. Otherwise it was calm right through until Saturday 14th July, when the army defences were removed. I remember watching from the kitchen window of the rectory, along with Olive, on Sunday 15th July at 6.00pm, as the army finally left the area after their operation of the previous week.

At this time the Weston Park talks failed in their attempt to break the impasse in the political process.

Drumcree Seven 2001 was a welcome change from the previous years. It was such a relief to have had a quiet and peaceful protest without any trouble.

I believe it was an answer to prayer. Many people have asked me why it was so calm at Drumcree in July 2001 and I have simply replied, "We prayed to God for a peaceful July and He heard our prayers and answered them." God has said, "Call upon me."

As July 2001 was left behind, with the problem still not resolved, I went ahead, believing that it would only be by prayer that a resolution would be found to the situation.

THE AUTUMN

As the autumn began there were still expectations that the Currin process would deliver a solution. However it was not to be because Portadown District LOL No1 declared on 8th November that they were completely finished with Currin. Once again I was disappointed about our lack of progress.

On 16th November I attended a meeting in the See House with the Archbishop, H. Gracey, D. Burrows, N.

Dawson, R. Monteith, D. Watson, J. Campbell and W. Bingham. It was decided to contact John Reid, Secretary of State for a meeting, but without success.

At the end of the year a new development in the issue came on 27th November, with the appointment of Sir George Quigley to carry out a review of the Parades Commission.[1]

---

1   The report was made in November 2002 recommending that the Parades Commission should have a "mediation" role (A Parades facilitation Agecny), as well as its "determinative" role.

Chapter 12

2002 Drumcree Eight

BEGINNING

THE new year began with two parades conferences being held on 28th January and 9th March in the Hilton Hotels at Templepatrick and Belfast, organised by the Community Relations Council, Incore and the Parades Commission, both of which I attended and found useful, because of the contacts I made with key people such as the Shadow Northern Ireland Secretary of State Quinten Davies, who on another occasion came to see me at the rectory and visited the church. The Conferences emphasised the need for LOL No1 to meet with the Parades Commission.

EARLY SPRING

A most pleasant occasion for Olive and me was when Sarah was married to Mervyn Cordner on 30th March in Drumcree Church. She was the first daughter of a serving rector to be married in Drumcree Church for at least 244 years. Drumcree was known for good news that day.

With Sarah, Mervyn and Olive

LATE SPRING

During the spring I attended a number of meetings with the Archbishop and the Officers of Portadown District LOL No 1 in such places as The See House, Church House, Drumcree Parochial Hall and Tartaraghan Parochial Hall, when there was talk about proximity talks which was a good idea and possible General Synod legislation to prevent a service being held, which seemed to me most unrealistic.

EARLY SUMMER

As July was speedily approaching, I was quite concerned that, while mediation had taken place, and many contacts had been made over a long period, between LOL No 1 and GRRC, nothing was being achieved. So I thought it might be worthwhile, as a clergyman, to approach the Roman Catholic clergy who ministered in the Garvaghy Road area and ask them if they would like to become involved in clerical attempts in mediation and the facilitation of dialogue, along with me. This had been attempted in 1996 by the Church leaders, but I thought it should be attempted again in 2002.

At the end of May I asked the clergy if they would contact Mr McKenna, Chairman of GRRC to set out the actual grievances the Coalition had concerning an Orange parade along the Garvaghy Road. Mr McKenna responded through the local clergy. The response was the ten points he had made to the Parades Commission, in July 2001. I conveyed this response to LOL No 1. Then LOL No 1 sent their reply to the Parades Commission to be conveyed to GRRC. This was a slow, tedious process, which I hoped would lead to progress, but the stalemate continued.

It was not my purpose to offer an opinion on a parade or objections to it. Nor was it my concern to comment on any response between the parties. I wanted simply to facilitate dialogue and assist in the shuttle of messages, which the Parades Commission called mediated dialogue.

JULY

The Parades Commission determination for the parade on Sunday 7th was given on Monday 1st. As expected the parade was banned from proceeding along Garvaghy Road.

LOL No 1 requested a review of the determination, so I telephoned Tony Holland on Wednesday 3rd and told him about my attempt at facilitating dialogue. However, in the review which was given on Friday 5th, while my approach was acknowledged, yet again the parade was banned.

The Parades Commission Review stated:

"In reviewing its decision, the Commission has again considered the information, advice and evidence received in relation to the parade, together with the further representations provided by Grand Lodge in its request for review, by GRRC and by Rev John Pickering, Rector of Drumcree Parish Church, about approaches he has made to the Garvaghy Road Residents Coalition through clerical intermediaries to find out GRRC concerns about the parade.

Having considered all the available information, we confirm our decision regarding the parade by Portadown District, LOL No 1 on Sunday 7th July 2002, detailed in the determination dated 1st July 2002."

It was a great disappointment.

Saturday 6th

At midday 6th July the security forces moved into the area around Drumcree and yet again erected a razor wire fence along the stream for a short distance. A small

Small barrier   *Olive Pickering*

barrier, only seven feet high, was erected on the road at the bridge.

I gave an interview about my approach to GRRC, (as I wanted to make it clear that efforts were being made to make progress), on Saturday afternoon 6th to Mervyn Jess of the BBC and he broadcast it on TV on Newsline at 5.30pm that evening.[1]

About 10.00pm that night a small fire was lit at the barrier by protesters, but it was of no consequence and was quickly put out. Then at 10.15pm four men arrived on the Hill carrying tyres and placed them at the barrier, but they were removed quickly by the police. The rest of that evening was quite peaceful.

Sunday 7th – Drumcree Sunday

When I arose at 7.00am I expected the day to be calm and peaceful, as I had been saying during the run up period. I checked the church at 7.30am and Alex Richardson was already at work connecting up the CCTV to the Parochial Hall for the broadcast of the service, while Robert Oliver arrived later to set up loud speakers outside for those who were unable to get into the Church or Parochial Hall.

Morning Service

I returned with Olive at 10.00am to be in good time for the

---

1 Belfast Telegraph Monday 8th July 2002
   Portadown Times, Friday 12th July 2002

service. It was not long until the parade arrived from Carleton Street Orange Hall, comprising 1,500 Orangemen and preceded by three bands. The service commenced promptly at 11.30am. I was assisted by Alan Barr, parish evangelist. The Lessons were read by Cecil Allen and George Robinson. Betty Best sang a solo entitled "Why Do You Wait", while my daughter Sarah Cordner played the organ and I preached the sermon about Jesus speaking to a great crowd assuring them of his help for their problems. The service went well with great reverence and much attention.

The Protest

After the service the Officers of Portadown District LOL No. 1 paraded to the barrier to make their protest to ACC Stephen White, PSNI[2] about the parade being banned from Garvaghy Road. I entered the field opposite the church and went along to the barrier, where I noticed that the District Officers were finding difficulty in making a clear space on the road, because of the huge crowd, as the ACC had to come forward to receive the protest. However, soon an area was made ready for the ACC to approach. Then I went across to the bank of the stream that ran along by the field. There I spoke with a number of unruly youths, who were throwing stones at the police on the bridge. I tried to persuade them to stop, but unfortunately

2   The RUC – Royal Ulster Constabulary had been renamed on 4th November 2001 to be the PSNI – The Police Service Northern Ireland

without success.   The Officers made their protest, speeches were made by Harold Gracey, David Burrows and Nigel Dawson, and then Cecil Allen said a prayer. After the District Officers returned up the Hill I left the field.

I entered the churchyard about 1.45pm by the main gate and went to the wall in the middle between the old ground and the terraced ground. There I observed the barrier had been broken and a confrontation between the police and the Orange was taking place, but I had a poor view of what was happening. It was not until I saw television pictures a few hours later that I became aware of how vicious attacks had been made upon the police. What happened was that the police had decided to put the large barricade of previous years in position. To do so the police needed to move the Orangemen slightly back from the bridge. As the police in full riot gear were preparing to move, some of the youths went in between the police and the Orange and carried out hand to hand fighting. At this point some of the less responsible Orangemen began to attack the police with stones and other missiles. The police responded by surging forward with a baton charge.

Meanwhile, as I was watching I saw the army putting the large barricade into position, which took a long time because they had misjudged the requirements of their measurements, and I became increasingly anxious. However, eventually the barrier was put in place, the police withdrew and calm was immediately restored. That was at about 2.20pm.

I discovered later that twenty-four police officers and a number of protestors had been injured. Arrests were made over the next few days and those arrested were remanded in custody.

The whole episode was most unfortunate. It was so disappointing after all the high hopes that there would be a peaceful protest.

David Burrows said, "We have called for a peaceful protest all along and we will continue to do so. We have marshals, but there is only so much that marshals can do. Some people don't want to listen to reasonable people so that is the difficulty we have."

ACC Stephen White said, "We were told it would be a dignified, law-abiding protest." Acknowledging that the police still had to be prepared for violence he said, "Unfortunately that is what happened. Mindless evil thugs attacked police officers."[3]

In the late afternoon I returned home for lunch with Olive, Sarah, Mervyn and Alan. At 4.00pm I went back to the Hill and was glad to find everything quiet, though still unaware of how bad the situation had been at 2.00pm.

About 4.30pm I had a conversation with the Archbishop, by telephone. He had started to get reports about the events, in which he said that it was quite possible that there would be people who would attribute

3   See News Letter 8 July 2002, p2.

blame to me for the horrible events of that day, because I had held the service. I was only trying to carry out my normal duties as a cleryman.

Evening Service

After watching many very distressing television pictures which much perturbed me I went to the 7.00pm service, also very upset at the suggestion of the Archbishop that the attribution of blame might be laid on me and I thought how it might lead to me being deprived of my parish. Alan Milligan, People's Churchwarden, commented, "You are looking very distressed this evening". Elizabeth Cochrane, Rector's churchwarden, suggested that the Archbishop should be invited to a meeting of the Select Vestry as soon as possible. Alan Barr conducted the service and I preached, though it was difficult to concentrate.

After the service I observed a little unrest. About 9.00pm I went out for a walk in the pouring rain to Corbracky Lane, pondering seriously the events of the day and the possible follow up, especially for myself. I met parishioners Sandra Courtney and June Cooper and family in a passing car, and they were kind enough to stop and bring me some encouragement.

Later, back at home, I observed a water cannon being used on the crowd, close to the barricade.

Despite the awful events of the day, and the feeling of having been let down by certain irresponsible individuals who had gone out of control, I resolved to work even harder for better days and managed to get a good night's sleep.

Monday 8th

The next day, Monday 8th July at 4.00pm a meeting of the Select Vestry with the Archbishop took place at the rectory. The Archbishop expressed concern at the perception of Drumcree Parish being associated with the violence of the previous day. It was underlined that this was simply a perception and reference was made to the statement which the Select Vestry had issued on the 13th September 2000, covering this point.

Nevertheless there was anxiety expressed by the Vestry about the possibility of the introduction of legislation in the General Synod 2003 to give power to bishops to cancel services. The members of the vestry were adamant that such a measure would seriously exacerbate the situation at Drumcree, because people would feel that not only were their civil liberties being threatened, but also their religious liberties.

I asked the Archbishop how this process would work out and what my position would be at the end of it. My conversation with the Archbishop went like this:-

I asked: "If such a law was passed what would happen then?"

The Archbishop replied: "I would be obliged to invoke the law, if I thought there would be violence. If I did not and others thought there may be violence, then I would be summoned to the Court of the General Synod and sacked."

Then I asked: "If you invoked the law against me, I would have to say that, despite having every respect for you, I would not obey the law. My position of not preventing anyone attending services, which is well stated, is because of my ordination vows and my conscience. What would happen to me then?"

The Archbishop said: "You would be summoned to the Court of the General Synod, (which I would refuse to chair because you belong to my diocese). You would lose the case and be deprived of your parish and perhaps not be allowed to have a licence in the Church of Ireland again and perhaps be defrocked.[4] You would be declared retired and in your case with a reduced pension which could be deferred for two years."

I said: "So be it."

Next I asked: "What could the General Synod do to the Select Vestry?"

The Archbishop responded: "Nothing."

As the meeting concluded I could not see the point of me being sacked and yet the service would still be held, as there was no bar on the Select Vestry making provision for services.

I never heard any more about the introduction of any legislation to cancel services. Indeed after my retirement,

---

4   The irony was that the unruly element who had fully supported me in keeping the church doors open, could be the cause of measures being brought in, which could lead to my dismissal!

three bishops approached me about giving me permission to officiate in their dioceses.

It was very interesting and helpful that the Church of Ireland Gazette in its Editorial of 12th July 2002 (which presumably was written on Monday 8th) said:

> "If he (John Pickering) was .... to refuse to hold the service........ (it) could lead to even greater trouble. The same would hold true if the Church of Ireland were to amend its law so that the service could be prohibited."

The Rest of the Week

During the next few days all was quiet. There were crowds of people present and the police monitored everyone who went up the Hill. The large barricade was replaced by the smaller one on Wednesday 10th and this caused a great deal of anxiety, as it had the possibility of encouraging rowdy people to attack it and cause a riot, but fortunately this did not happen.

When Saturday 13th July arrived the army removed all fortifications and by mid-afternoon everything was back to normal at Drumcree.

PETITION TO THE ARCHBISHOP

News of my possible dismissal left the parishioners very disturbed, so during the summer 616 parishioners signed a petition, organised by Gary Miller and the Churchwardens Elizabeth Cochrane and Alan Milligan. It was delivered to the Archbishop on Monday 7th October by the Churchwardens along with Gary Miller.

The petition was in support of my principled stand, my policy of an open church door for everyone. It also supported the importance of resisting any change to the laws of the Church of Ireland, whereby a bishop would be given authority to cancel church services. The Petition gave me great strength and encouragement in my stand and much hope that the laws of the Church would remain unchanged.

The End of the Year

The Assembly was suspended on 15th October because of the Stormontgate affair, in which the PSNI raided the Sinn Fein offices at Stormont and found classified material on computers including the addresses of police officers.

Paul Murphy (Labour) was appointed Northern Ireland Secretary of State on 23rd October.

Chapter 13
2003 Drumcree Nine

DURING the earlier part of the year I was not aware of any efforts being made to help with a solution to the Drumcree problem, which was very frustrating. The Parades Commission was re-appointed in February.

On 1st May Tony Blair, called off the expected elections to the Northern Ireland Assembly, which had ended on 30th April (having been suspended since October 2002), because the IRA had not satisfied him that all paramilitary activity would end, all arms be given up and that the war would be declared over.

On Sunday 29th May, newspapers reported a plan that was said to involve an agreement between Portadown LOL No 1 and GRRC for a parade, with talks taking place beforehand and further parades being subject to consent. However, by Drumcree Sunday nothing had become of it.

JULY

Saturday 5th

The army commenced putting their fortifications into place at 8.00 am. I watched from the rectory as they began to put razor wire across the fields along the stream for a short distance. Also they put a small eight feet high, steel, black and yellow barrier on the bridge, which I thought was totally inadequate should trouble arise at any time. However, a large barricade was kept in reserve in

Army preparations   *Kelvin Boyes/Presseye*

Preparations continue   *Kelvin Boyes/Presseye*

the background. A small group came to observe the fortifications.

SUNDAY 6th - DRUMCREE SUNDAY

I made an early rise around 6.30 am on Sunday 6th, because it was Drumcree Sunday. I could scarcely believe as I looked out across the fields from the rectory that once again the army and police were in position with their fortifications in preparation for whatever the day might bring.

At 7.30 am the Orange Officers: David Burrows, Nigel Dawson and George Robinson along with Alan Milligan arrived and began to cordon off a section of the road in front of the barrier, with a length of tape, to delineate an area to be clear of people, to make it easier for the protest letter to be handed to the police.

Alex Richardson was already at work installing the CCTV link to the Parochial Hall, while Robert Oliver had installed loudspeakers outside the previous Friday.

Olive and I went to the church at 10.00am. Some people had already arrived, although not as many as in previous years. I made my final preparations for the service.

The parade left Carleton Street Orange Hall at 10.15am. The parade, accompanied by the Star of David and Edgarstown Accordion bands, was fewer in number this year, with about 1,000 brethren.

The parade arrived at the church at 11.15am. The church was filled and the overflow was accommodated in the Parochial Hall. The rest stood outside the church and the Hall joining in the service, as it was relayed outside to them.

At the beginning of the service I said, "Drumcree, which means a 'ridge of the branch', has grown into a symbol of the difference there is between the two sides of what may be called the ridge of Northern Ireland, with its difference of outlook and division between two identities or branches of people." I called upon the congregation to have confidence in God that Drumcree would become a symbol of agreement and healing for the people of this country. Then I drew attention to the fact that everyone was mindful of those who had served at the Battle of the Somme, which had begun on 1 July, 1916.

The service was conducted by Captain Alan Barr. The Lessons were read by Cecil Allen and George Robinson, while Wilson Sharpe sang a solo entitled "Father Almighty". The congregation was very attentive to the sermon which I preached about Jesus giving fullness of life. I expressed optimism for the future. The service was uplifting with good singing and a wonderful sense of the presence of God.

After the service the brethren paraded to the barrier where Nigel Dawson, handed a letter of protest to PSNI ACC Jonathan McIvor. Then Nigel Dawson said, "Remove this hideous barrier and your men."[1] Then there was Scripture reading and prayer. Having been refused their parade, the brethren returned to the top of the Hill where David Burrows, addressed the crowd and said, "We will continue to stand here until our rights are given back to us."[2] The media, whose presence had not been as obvious this year, certainly made up for that at this point, by appearing in a great number with cameras, tape recorders and notebooks.

After the singing of the National Anthem, the crowd dispersed quickly and quietly. Harold Gracey, who was recovering from his second hip operation, had to remain seated in a car at this time. I stood beside him as he spoke out of the car window to journalists saying, "I am completely behind Portadown District in all that they are doing to find a solution to this problem."

The whole event was perfectly peaceful and absolutely calm, with no trouble whatsoever, the calmest Drumcree

1   News Letter 7 July 2003, p4.
2   News Letter 7 July 2003, p4.

Sunday since before 1995. I was so thankful to God that everything passed off peacefully. A few people remained on the Hill[3] on Sunday evening.

Monday 7th and Tuesday 8th

A number of people gathered on the Hill again on Monday evening. When I rose just before 8.00am on Tuesday morning and looked out my bedroom window, while Olive still slept, I saw the army removing the barrier from the bridge and knew that Drumcree Nine had come to an end.

However, I knew that efforts would have to continue to find a solution.

Saturday 12th

Olive and I attended the Twelfth Demonstration in Markethill and had an enjoyable day. By now Portadown LOL No 1 had well-established the practice of carrying their substitute bannerette with the words, "Our Bannerette is still at Drumcree."

November

Assembly elections were held on 26th November at which the UUP lost out from being the largest party to the DUP, because of growing opposition to the Good Friday Agreement. Changes were coming about in politics, but it was hard to see it affecting the Drumcree situation.

3   News Letter 7 July 2003, p1

Chapter 14

2004 Drumcree Ten

SOUTH AFRICA TRIP

2004 began with the Parades Commission making plans for a "study trip conference" in South Africa in February, to study conflict resolution. Taking part would be the Parades Commission and representatives of various interests in the Portadown area including LOL No 1, GRRC, PSNI, CRC, Portadown 2000 and clergy. The aim was to find a way forward towards a resolution of the Drumcree problem.

The plan was leaked on BBC TV on Friday 9th January. Later that day I received a phone call from the Parades Commission inviting me to join those going on the study trip.

I felt that the idea was good, but I reckoned that I needed more information to ascertain whether the "study trip" would be worthwhile. I visited the Parades Commission secretariat the following Wednesday 14th January and met the Commission on Thursday 15th January to be fully acquainted with the project. From what I was told I was satisfied that the "study trip" would be worthwhile and so I accepted the invitation.

Nothing seemed to be happening for a while, until I received a message on Saturday 7th February that I would be departing for the "study trip" on Wednesday 11th February.

There was very little time to make preparation. Olive hurried around the house and rushed about the town over the next two days, getting me organised. Sandals had to be fitted on, sun cream and insect repellant obtained, a sun hat located, summer clothes hastily retrieved from winter storage, bottles of water purchased and a quick visit made to Dr. David Dorman at 8.00am one morning before the trip for an injection to protect me from tropical diseases.

When Wednesday 11th February came I waved goodbye to Olive at 12 noon as I climbed into Ian Milne's big car to be transported to Belfast City Airport with David Burrows. There, others were waiting to travel to

Heathrow, from where the group took off on an eleven hour flight to Johannesburg. The group consisted of Jim Rea, then of Portadown Methodist Church and me, clergy, David Burrows and Nigel Dawson, LOL No 1, Diane Hunniford of Portadown 2000, Ray Mullen, CRC, Irwin Turbitt and Alan McCrum, PSNI., Peter Osborne, John Cousins, Andrew Elliott, Ronnie Pedlow, Gordon Douglas and Stephen Kelly of the Parades Commission, with Brian Currin acting as facilitator.

The study trip "conference" began on Thursday 12th, when there was a series of seminars taken by leading personalities from across the South African political spectrum. They had been involved in conflict resolution in South Africa, during the time when it was on the brink of civil war in the years leading up to 1994, when apartheid was dismantled and a settlement for peace was agreed. While there has been much progress achieved, much work remains to be done. Though there is ostentatious wealth, as is seen in such places as Sandton with its grandeur, there is also abject poverty in some black areas, as I witnessed in such places as the informal settlement of Alexandra, where about three million inhabitants are crammed into a very small area, living in appalling squalid conditions. However, the people there were well dressed, pleasant and polite, but there are huge problems because of a lack of proper housing, services and employment. Drug trafficking, crime and corruption are very serious problems in South Africa and much needs to be done to deal with these evils.

Despite these issues the infrastructure of the country is excellent and travel is easy.

At that time of year the weather was pleasantly warm as it was the end of summer. The wild life, beautiful scenery and the night sky were marvellous to experience too.

I had a most uplifting experience when I attended a crowded service of worship with powerful music and singing and a stirring sermon in Johannesburg Central Methodist Church on the Sunday morning of my visit to that city.

Re-routed   *John Pickering*

However, there was work to be done. The conference developed into more intensive in-depth study, with long sessions in the quietness of the Sediba Game Park Reserve from Monday until Thursday.

I believe that this was a great new turn in events of Drumcree, because representatives of Portadown LOL No 1, David Burrows and Nigel Dawson, met with members of the Parades Commission for the first time. This was right and good to do. It would not always have been advisable to do so, but as circumstances had changed and the Parades Commission showed a willingness to listen to the Orange it was the proper thing for the Orange to meet with them. I believe that this meeting was most beneficial, as was the whole conference for developing relationships. It is difficult to know why Grand Lodge opposed the attendance of the Portadown brethren at the conference. In the changed circumstances I believe Grand Lodge should have appreciated the value of meeting with the Parades Commission. Besides, members of the Orange Order had begun to meet with the Commission, wearing other 'hats'. It was a pity that the GRRC did not accept the invitation to attend the conference, as they were continually asking to have talks with LOL No 1. It is difficult to understand why they failed to take this opportunity.

I admit I was quite exhausted as the conference concluded on Friday 20th February. After a return eleven hour flight the plane arrived in Heathrow the next morning, and after a short flight to Belfast I reached home, after a very useful, educational and interesting visit.

There was a useful follow up to the conference at the Green Gables Hotel, Hillsborough for assessment on

Thursday 13th May, with all the participants and John Carrick, a newly elected LOL officer of great promise, who was also present.

ALABAMA VISIT

2004 was to be a year of travel as Olive and I had the wonderful privilege of visiting the State of Alabama in the United States of America during March that year.

It came about because the Very Rev. Dr. Paul Zahl, Dean of the Cathedral Church of the Advent in Birmingham City centre, while on a visit to Ireland in July 2001, had liked an account of my sermon on Drumcree Sunday in the News Letter, in which I had said that no matter how many barriers there were in life, there is hope by trust in the Lord Jesus Christ. He invited me to speak at some of his Lenten Noonday Services, to share my experience of Drumcree, and to bring Olive, with all expenses paid. In April 2002 definite arrangements were made for the visit to take place in 2004.

I was very pleased to go and preach at two Lenten Services on Thursday 25th and Friday 26th March 2004. My visit included some other speaking engagements, among which was a very memorable meeting, with a newly-formed Orange Lodge, the Sons of William No 1003, named after a lodge of that name in Maghera, Co. Londonderry. Among the brethren, led by its Master, Michael Cooper, were quite a number of members of the legal profession. Because of worldwide interest in

Drumcree, BBC reporter Ann Dawson was also present for the programme 'Sunday Sequence' and she concurred with what I said, which was very supportive to me.

The warmth of the welcome from Paul and his lovely wife Mary and everyone else, and their outgoing friendship during the visit, was absolutely overwhelming. Olive and I were most thankful for the privilege of that visit to Alabama, by which our lives were so greatly enriched.

While I was away the death took place of Harold Gracey, on Sunday 28th March. This was very sad for LOL No, 1 as Harold had played such a leading role in the protest. I returned home just in time to attend his funeral in Seagoe Parish Church on Tuesday 30th March and I preached at a Memorial Service for Harold in Drumcree Parish Church on Sunday 5th September.

JUNE

The month of June seemed to come upon me quicker than usual in 2004. It began with a meeting for an update on the situation, with the Archbishop, David Burrows (now Portadown LOL No 1 District Master), Nigel Dawson (now Portadown Deputy Master) and Richard Monteith on 1st June. I had a meeting with the Parades Commission on 23rd June, and they said that engagement must take place with GRRC by direct or indirect means.

On the last Sunday in June a Sunday newspaper reported that Grand Lodge had decided to suspend

Portadown District LOL No 1 from membership of the Orange Order, because of their visit to South Africa, subject to consultation with the Armagh County Lodge. However, Portadown LOL No 1 had not received any communication from Grand Lodge or the County Armagh Lodge, which was rather a mystery.

JULY

The Parades Commission determination for the parade on Sunday 4th July was issued on Thursday 24th June and as usual it was re-routed from Garvaghy Road. Portadown LOL No 1 requested a review of the determination, but this was refused and they were annoyed because they understood that Belfast District LOL No. 9 was granted a review on 26th June for their Annual Whiterock Parade. I decided to phone Tony Holland, Chairman of the Parades Commission and ask for mediation to be put into place, but it was not arranged.

The week prior to the Drumcree parade was quiet, such a welcome change from most of the previous years. On Saturday morning 3rd July the army moved into the area around the church and began putting security measures in place, which included a small barrier with gates on the bridge, and a row of razor wire along the stream. As usual some people came to observe in the morning and afternoon and there were quite a number of people present by evening who remained until midnight.

Sunday 4th – Drumcree Sunday

I rose at 6.00am and began making preparations for the day ahead. At 7.45am I went to the Hill and viewed the security measures in place and the security forces on duty.

At 8.30am PSNI officers, accompanied by John Wilson, set up a check point at the first road junction between the rectory and the church. I returned to the rectory for breakfast, and to make final preparations. At 10.30 a.m. Olive and I set off for the service. The parade arrived at the church from Carleton Street Orange Hall at 11.15am, comprising about 900 Orangemen, led by Edgarstown and the Star of David bands.[1]

The service commenced at 11.30 am. I welcomed everyone, while Captain Alan Barr conducted the service and Wilson Sharpe sang a solo entitled "Before the Throne of God Above". Cecil Allen and George Robinson read the Lessons, and Wendy Walsh played the organ. I said the prayers and preached the sermon, which was about Paul's message on the hill at Athens, calling his hearers to trust in God. Everyone was very attentive and receptive to what was being said and sung. There was a very sincere and reverent atmosphere of worship throughout the service.

At the end of the service David Burrows spoke in the church expressing appreciation for the service. When the brethren left the church they formed up on the road and

---

1 The media wanted to know why the numbers were fewer than in previous years. But in reality they were normal for the pre 1995 parades. I did chuckle at the media's questioning of the numbers, because in the years when there were large numbers, the media wanted to know why the numbers were so large!

paraded to the barrier to make their usual protest about not being allowed to parade on Garvaghy Road back to the Orange Hall in Carleton Street, Portadown. A tape had been put across the road at the lower gate to create space for the officers of Portadown District to meet the PSNI and make their protest. A short service was then held, conducted by Cecil Allen. A silence was observed for the late Harold Gracey, and everyone returned to the top of the Hill to disperse.

Immediately the army began to dismantle and remove the fortifications. The whole morning was perfectly quiet and absolutely peaceful, for which I thanked Almighty God. ACC Jonathan McIvor said he was delighted the parade had passed off peacefully.

The following morning's News Letter reflected on the peace and the future, quoting Dr. Arthur Cassidy, a QUB researcher, who said, "From a Christian perspective, people will have to move beyond politics and think in terms of human desires, anxiety and fears". And so July 2004, along with July 2003, proved to be the best years since 1994. The army finally cleared up on Monday morning and I watched as they left at 9.00am.

However, as the problem was still not resolved, I decided that very afternoon to try to keep things moving by asking the Parades Commission for mediation to commence again as soon as possible. Still nothing happened.

During the Autumn a conference was held in Leeds Castle to get movement in the peace process, but it did not accomplish much because of lack of time.

A reasonably quiet year in Northern Ireland was shattered when the Northern Bank in Belfast was raided of £26.5m on Tuesday 21st December. The IRA was blamed and so the peace process was set back yet again.

Chapter 15

2005 Drumcree Eleven

EARLY DAYS

THE year began with the IRA issuing a statement on Wednesday 2nd February at 9.00pm in which they said that they had withdrawn from a scheme to put its arms permanently beyond use. The next day the IRA issued a second statement which said "Do not underestimate the seriousness of the situation". The consequence was that the Northern Ireland Peace Plan of Good Friday 1998 was put on hold.

LATE SPRING

During the late spring, on 5th May, a General Election was held and David Trimble UUP, who had played a big part in the early days of the Drumcree problem, lost his seat as MP for the Upper Bann Constituency to David Simpson DUP, because of his support for the Good Friday Agreement. Subsequently Trimble resigned as Leader of the Ulster Unionist Party.   Peter Hain (Labour) was appointed Northern Ireland Secretary of State. Although the political scene was changing, still nothing was happening as regards solving the Drumcree situation.

In the period before Drumcree Sunday welcome calmness prevailed all the time, without any of the hype and anxiety of the previous years. However the Parades Commission ruled against the parade.

On a personal level it was an anxious time for Sarah and me when Olive was diagnosed with cancer of the throat on Friday 17th June.

JULY

Sunday 10th - Drumcree Sunday

When Drumcree Sunday came, which was Sunday 10th July, activity began at 3.00am with the army putting a barrier in place at the bridge beyond the church. The barrier was different from former years. This time it consisted of two black gates with yellow pillars. The gates

Gates and small barrier   *Olive Pickering*

remained open most of the time. In front of the gates zinc crush barriers were put in place in squares. Razor wire was strewn along the bottom of the first field beyond the bridge, but altogether security measures were scaled down.

The Orange Parade of over 600 brethren which left Carleton Street 10.15am arrived at Drumcree Church at 11.15am, once more accompanied by Edgarstown Accordian Band and the Star of David Accordian Band.

The service was conducted by Cecil Allen, LOL No 1 District Chaplain and Church of Ireland Lay Reader. The Lessons were read by Sandy Hewitt and George Robinson LOL No 1 District Chaplains. Wilson Sharpe sang a solo. Wendy Walsh played the organ.

During the service there was a minute's silence to remember those who died a the Battle of the Somme in the two World Wars and other conflicts, including the Troubles. The service also marked the National Day of Celebration to commemorate the sixtieth Anniversary of VE/VJ Day. In my sermon based on Proverbs 29 v 18, "Where there is no vision the people perish", I exhorted the congregation to have a vision for the future. I said, "Many have experienced broken dreams about the parading issue, the governance of the country, the peace of the world and satisfaction in their own lives. What people need is to be built up with vision for a good future, by trust in God though Jesus Christ".

Because agreement was reached in Londonderry, that for the first time in thirteen years, five districts of County Londonderry LOL would be able to parade in Londonderry city centre, I said, "Vision and imagination have been used in the situation in Londonderry and the parade has been rescued on the 12th July. Why can something like this not be done elsewhere, why not here at Drumcree?"

My sermon was widely reported in the media by them saying that I had called for dialogue between the Orange Order and nationalist residents. At the conclusion of the service the District Master David Burrows paid tribute to me and the Select Vestry.

Following the church service officials from the Orange Lodge walked to the security barrier, where there were five police officers, to formally protest to PSNI about the Parades Commission's decision to once again ban the annual parade from walking down the Garvaghy Road.

Protest in rain   *Portadown Times*

Expressing "disgust and disappointment" on behalf of the local Orangemen and women, David Jones (Portadown District Secretary) heaped criticism on both the PSNI and the Parades Commission. Addressing Superintendent Robbie Pedlow at the gates Mr Jones asked the officer to, "take back to the Parades Commission Portadown District's resolve to remain at this particular place until such time as we can parade peacefully down the Garvaghy Road". He added, "Our resolve is as strong as it was in 1998. We will be back next Sunday, the following Sunday and the Sunday after that until such time as our parade is able to go down the Garvaghy Road". A small group lingered at the security gates in defiance of a Parades Commission ruling which determined that Drumcree Hill should be cleared by 2.30pm. PSNI

Superintendent Drew Harris said he was satisfied with the good way things had gone.

Thankfully the whole day passed by peacefully and the barrier was removed by 6.00pm.

RESIGNATION

The shock resignation of David Burrows as LOL No 1 District Master was announced on Friday 22nd July and it brought me great sadness as I had a very close working relationship with him. Daryl Hewitt was appointed District Master.

IRA STATEMENT

The leadership of the IRA formally ordered an end to their armed campaign, as from Thursday 28th July at 4.00pm. This marked the end of over thirty years of the Troubles. This meant that progress could now be made towards the implementation of the Good Friday Agreement.

As regards Drumcree, however, nothing seemed to be happening throughout the rest of the year, so I was able to concentrate on my parochial duties. Olive began to undergo treatment at that time.

Chapter 16
2006 Drumcree Twelve

JANUARY - JUNE

THE year 2006 began with the appointment on 1st January (named on 1st December 2005) of entirely new members to the Parades Commission, as follows: Roger Poole (Chairman), Alison Scott-McKinley, Joe Hendron, Anne Monaghan, Vilma Patterson, Donald MacKay soon to be replaced by Kelly Andrews and to everyone's great surprise, David Burrows, who subsequently resigned from the Orange Order and in due course had his membership of the Parades Commission ruled unlawful because he had been a member of the Orange Order. He was replaced by Irena Shephard.

In the spring on Thursday 6th April, Tony Blair and Bertie Ahern announced that if devolved government was not set up in Northern Ireland by 24th November 2006, the Assembly would be wound up and they would have to find a different way forward. They hoped this would create the necessary impetus to find a solution to the differences between the political parties.

Meanwhile, things at Drumcree remained unchanged, but at home Sarah and I were trying to cope with the deterioration in Olive's state of health. Sadly, while it was thought that Olive was overcoming cancer of her throat and also her neck, her lungs were discovered to have taken up the disease, followed by her liver. For Olive's type of cancer there was no cure. She was nursed most lovingly in Newry Hospice, where she died on Easter Sunday 16th April. Olive's passing has been a great loss for me and it made a huge difference to my life, as my chief earthly comfort had gone, but with the help of God I have been living one day at a time and coping well with life.

JULY

Sunday 9th – Drumcree Sunday

The Parades Commission again ruled against the parade. When Drumcree Twelve came around in July 2006, it turned out to be the quietest July since 1994, the year before the stand-offs began.

The day began with LOL No. 1 parading from Carleton Street Orange Hall as usual. There was no immediate army presence and that was the first time since 1995. There was also a significant drop in the number of PSNI officers on the ground. The parade was led by Armagh County Grand Master Denis Watson, Roger Gardiner Armagh County Secretary, Darryl Hewitt and the other Officers of Portadown District LOL No 1. For the first time a new ex-servicemen's standard, commemorating the Battle of the Somme and the Battle of the Diamond, was carried at the front of the parade by Johnny Gray of the Ex-Servicemen's Lodge No. 608.

The Service, with 535 in attendance, including an overflow, commenced at 11.30 am. There was a special commemoration for the ninetieth anniversary of the Battle of the Somme in 1916 and everyone wore poppies.

The Service was conducted by Mr Cecil Allen. The Lessons were read by George Robinson and Sandy Hewitt while the soloist was Betty Best.

I began my sermon by saying, "As you parade today the question needs to be asked, What is required of LOL No 1 for their parade to be completed?' In the sermon I referred to the parade as a journey. On a spiritual level I reminded the worshippers that they were on the difficult journey of life and I urged them to follow the Lord Jesus Christ.

After the service the Orangemen paraded to the barrier at the bridge at the end of the churchyard, and the Officers made a verbal protest to the PSNI, represented by

Nigel Dawson. Darryl Hewitt said, "We will continue to protest every Sunday in an attempt to parade along Garvaghy Road to Portadown." Also he called for the resignation of the Protestant members of the Parades Commission. All was perfectly calm for which we were profoundly thankful to Almighty God. Superintendent Alan Todd later said, "This has been a positive day for the whole of Portadown."[1] But I did miss Olive and her support very much that day.

AUTUMN

The St. Andrews Agreement was made on 13th October to get the Northern Ireland Assembly started. Also it was decided to have a review of the Parades Commission.

Importantly in October, Portadown LOL No 1 had a rethink about their policy of refusing to talk directly face to face with the GRRC and they concluded that the time was now right for them to enter into face-to-face dialogue with them. LOL No 1 informed the Parades Commission of their decision, expecting the Commission to facilitate talks without any delay. However, delay there was, to the bitter disappointment of LOL No 1, and by the end of the year no direct talks had been arranged.

I was very dismayed that there were no talks after all the calls since 1998 for LOL No 1 to take part in direct talks. It seemed that the Parades Commission were willing to allow matters to continue as they were – the parade

1   Belfast Telegraph 10 July 2006

being formally refused their traditional route back to Portadown and the Orange leaders making a formal but peaceful protest against it! Perhaps it suited the "powers that be" that things should continue in that same "routine", which had to be endured at Drumcree for so many years.

On 24th November Ian Paisley, DUP, agreed to become First Minister and Martin McGuinness, SF, Deputy First Minister. Political changes were going ahead, so why could the Parades Commission not make an effort to progress.

Chapter 17
2007 Drumcree Thirteen

SPRING

ALL during the springtime Portadown LOL No 1 waited expectantly for the Parades Commission to put in place mechanisms for direct face-to-face talks to take place between LOL No 1 and the GRRC, but nothing was arranged.

Portadown LOL No 1 was at a great loss to understand why the Parades Commission, which had continually urged them to enter into direct dialogue with GRRC, was not taking action to implement talks, now that LOL No 1 had changed its mind about direct dialogue.

Furthermore LOL No 1 could not understand it when they heard that Brendan McKenna, Chairperson of GRRC, refused the offer of entering into direct dialogue with them, after everything he had said over the past ten years about wishing to have face-to-face talks and continually seeking to encourage such talks, as the way forward in the parading issue.

Assembly elections were held on the 7th March but David Trimble did not stand. This brought an end to his direct involvement in Northern Ireland politics after being so prominent since 1995.

LOL No 1 was greatly dismayed as they approached the summer that their offer of face-to-face talks was still not acted upon, in spite of a widespread wish that they enter talks.

In April "The Strategic Review of Parades Body" was set up under the chairmanship of Lord Ashdown. The Orange Order welcomed this review because they saw it as leading to the scrapping of the Parades Commission. The Body recommended that the Parades Commission should cease and District Councils become involved in the Parading issue from 2009 and this was agreed to by the government.

On 8th May the Northern Ireland Assembly Executive was restored with Rev. Ian Paisley as First Minister and Mr Martin McGuinness as Deputy First Minister. But there was still no change with the Drumcree issue.

JUNE

My retirement as Rector of Drumcree Parish after twenty four years and full-time ministry after forty two years, which I announced at morning service in Drumcree Church on Sunday 15th April, to take effect on 30th September 2007, was taken up by the media from the end of June onwards. Writing in the Belfast Telegraph on 27th June Alf McCreery said that I was retiring from "one of the most controversial posts in the Irish Church." In the News Letter on Thursday 28th June Laura Murphy said that I had "offered a witness through some difficult years." Judith Cole presented a very pleasing tribute to Olive in the Belfast Telegraph on Thursday 12th July and recalled my position at Drumcree, being so ably supported by Olive.

Mr Shaun Woodward was appointed Secretary of State for Northern Ireland at the beginning of July.

JULY

Sunday 8th - Drumcree Sunday

Yet again the Parades Commission decided against the parade. According to custom, at the beginning of July, Portadown District LOL No 1 paraded from Carleton Street Orange Hall to Drumcree Parish to attend morning worship. It was very pleasing that there was not any hint of trouble along the route. The PSNI presence was at a minimum.

That year was very special because it was the two hundredth anniversary of the first Orange Parade Service held at Drumcree Parish Church in 1807, and I dedicated an oak lectern, presented by LOL No 1 to the church to commemorate the event. Maybe it marked a significant time for me to retire. The church was packed to capacity for the service. As usual there was an overflow of people, who joined in the service by relay in the Parochial Hall and outside. Assisting me at the service was Cecil Allen. The Lessons were read by George Robinson and Sandy Hewitt. Wilson Sharpe sang a solo, while the organist was Wendy Walsh.   Once more, those who died at the Battle of the Somme were commemorated, especially those who were from County Armagh and County Monaghan.

In my sermon I concentrated upon the word "last", as I would be retiring soon. 1 started by commenting "I find it hard to believe that the Orange Parade which has taken place, in 1997 was to be the *last* parade returning to Carleton Street", and mentioned that this was my *last* Orange Service sermon in Drumcree. Then I drew the attention of the congregation to a sobering fact when I said, "One day you will attend your *last* Orange Service and listen to your *last* Orange sermon and have your *last* opportunity to respond to the gospel and maybe that is today." I exhorted my hearers to respond positively to the Word of God by trusting in Jesus Christ as Lord and Saviour for the good of their lives each day and forever.

After the service the brethren paraded in pouring rain to the scaled-down barrier consisting of metal gates, where about twelve PSNI officers were waiting. David Jones made a formal protest. Then Darryl Hewitt told Orangemen and dozens of reporters, "Let there be no doubt, we are committed to face-to-face talks under an independent chairman with no pre-conditions." The Parades Commission had, in his view, failed to take any action since the Order requested unconditional face-to-face talks with the residents nine months before. "Constantly we have been told the only way to resolve any dispute is dialogue," said Mr Hewitt. He added "The Garvaghy Road Residents Coalition have consistently demanded dialogue. My question today is 'Who is refusing to talk now? Most reasonable people would, I assume, agree that nine months is a more than adequate time scale for a process to start." Mr Hewitt added: "Some

Formal protest   *Portadown Times*

would have us believe that there is a new political dispensation. For some that might be true. However, as we stand here today in front of this metal barrier we must ask the question - when will this political dispensation apply to the rights of freedom of the Orange Brethren standing here at Drumcree Hill?"

Thankfully once more the whole day was a very peaceful one. PSNI Chief Superintendent Alan Todd praised the Order for their peaceful parade, and there was a great mood of optimism that a resolution to the Drumcree problem might be in sight.

RETIREMENT

It was not easy to retire from what was my whole way of life, and with the Drumcree situation unresolved, but when the day to retire comes it must be accepted. Parish life, which had continued its normal pattern through all the protests, would carry on, as before.

I am so grateful to the parishioners for arranging such a marvellous farewell for me the evening before I retired and a supper after my final service, at which I was overwhelmed with the large number of people who attended to give me good wishes for the future. I will always be full of gratitude to the parish and parish organisations for the very useful and valuable gifts that they gave me, and to Portadown LOL No 1 for the Bible and monetary gift that they presented to me.

The Portadown Times on 5th October 2007, penned a very apt conclusion for me by saying, "Then on Sunday night Mr Pickering preached at his final service, enjoyed a parish supper in the Parochial Hall and went home to the rectory for his final night. The removal men came on Monday and the Pickering era at the Church of the Ascension, Drumcree, officially ended."

Retirement presentation   *Sarah Cordner*

PART THREE

Reflections

Reflections

As I reflect upon my time at Drumcree and all that has happened there, excluding July 2008, Drumcree Fourteen, which I did not witness, I am struck by the many issues that it raised – that of civil freedom, religious freedom, its position within the Church of Ireland, the role of the media and, perhaps most difficult of all, my own role there.

Chapter 18
Drumcree and Civil Freedom

FOR at least half of my life there has been strong conflict in Northern Ireland between the two sections of the community. This conflict, at its simplist, is about a clash between the unionists, generally Protestants, who uphold maintaining the union with Great Britain, and the nationalists, generally Roman Catholics, who aspire towards an all Ireland state.

As the conflict continued each section of people felt increasingly that *their* cultural, political and religious rights and way of life were being curtailed and indeed threatened by the other section of people. So a sense of alienation, insecurity and a lack of trust abounded.

It had been reckoned that the conflict was going to be expressed decisively somewhere in the country, and *that* place happened to be Drumcree. The timing happened to be from 1995 onwards when Portadown LOL No1 was prevented by the GRRC from parading along Garvaghy Road to Carleton Street Orange Hall after their annual attendance at morning service in Drumcree Parish Church in July each year. At Drumcree there was an outward manifestation of the differences and divisions that had been increasing over many years. Drumcree became a microcosm and cameo of the political problems of Northern Ireland.

As is well known now this conflict was expressed in a visible, tangible, material, physical and emotional manner, in the vociferous protest by LOL No 1 in the form of their stand-off with GRRC and the RUC, because to make an attack upon a parade us seen as a serious attack on the Protestant religion, culture and way of life.[1]

The protest which was strongly supported by brethren throughout the country and beyond, grew very quickly and enormously.

It became very clear to me during the latter part of that first day of the stand-off that there were serious political implications to the events that were taking place before my eyes, and I said so on a Radio Ulster interview

1   See Hastings Donnan & Graham McFarlane "Culture and Policy of Northern Ireland" – Institute of Irish Studies (QUB, 1997) p223

on Monday 10th July 1995 at 7.40am. I observed that at the stand-off, as well as it being an expression of the Orange Order's objection to not being allowed to parade from Drumcree to Portadown, along the Garvaghy Road, it was also demonstrating its increasing opposition to, as they saw it, their Protestant identity and political way of life being curtailed and ignored over many years.

Many authors and journalists have commented on this aspect of civil freedom. Clifford Smith, the Orange historian, says of Robert Moss, who published "Urban Guerillas" in 1972, "he foresaw Drumcree a long way off".[2] Gerry Adams told a Sinn Fein conference in Athboy in November 1996, "Three years of work went into creating that situation".[3]

Harvey Cox, Professor of History at Harvard University says that the Orange felt "their way of life is under siege". He says the fact that "complex political, economic and demographic forces [which] were operating since the 1960's mean that this sense is well founded".[4]

This point is well put by Thomas Hennesey, "These fears had crystallised during the marching season at the 'Siege of Drumcree', in July 1995, when a stand-off occurred, with Orangemen initially prevented from marching through what they considered a traditional route, which passed along the mainly nationalist Garvaghy Road in Portadown. Unionists felt that their

2   Clifford Smith, "The Vision" pg 133
3   Brian Kennaway, "The Orange Order (Methuen, 2006) p90
4   Marianne Elliott (Ed.), "The Long Road to Peace in NI" (Liverpool, 2007) p164

political rights had been taken from them now their cultural rights were being eroded."[5]

The Belfast Telegraph said very concisely in its Editorial on Monday 10th July 1995:

> "The stand-off between Orange Order members and police in Portadown is not just about a march route. It is about one community saying that compromise has gone far enough. Unionists feel they have to make too many concessions in the peace process and the prelude to it. The seeds of this demonstration were sown in the Anglo-Irish Agreement (15 November 1985) and the Downing Street Declaration (15 December 1993) and the Frameworks Document (22 February 1995),
> Yet it is those agreements which drive nationalists towards seeking even more concessions. They have seen the political tide flow in their favour and are demanding equality of status, never mind parity of esteem. Just as the demography of NI was redrawn by violence, so the political boundaries are being fought over in peacetime.
> The peace process is at a very fragile juncture. It is easy to exhort the two communities towards compromise, but it is difficult to put those words into practice. A fearful unionist community, faced with a determined and demanding nationalist community, is in no mood to make political

5   Thomas Hennessey, "The NI Peace Process" (Gill and Macmillan 2000) p97

concessions, which are perceived as a threat to the union. Similarly nationalists, believing that continual pressure is the only way of gaining parity, are reluctant to ease off on their demands."

Paul Bew, Professor of Irish Politics at Queens University said, "The confrontation in Portadown was a product of a general unionist lack of faith in British intentions".[6]

In early 1997 John A. Murphy, sometime Professor of History at University College Dublin, saw it as 'obvious' that as long as there was appeasement of Sinn Fein/IRA, the terrorists would continue to apply pressure on both governments until their long term objective was achieved. He said, "At present such pressure is being applied to get Sinn Fein into talks, then it will be used to promote cross border institutions, after that to force the pace to a united Ireland, next to move towards a 'socialist' (really a fascist) republic".[7]

As David Trimble said to the Independent on 10th July 1998, "Our culture is being crushed". The Portadown Times, reflecting in 2001 in a leading article, said well, "The past six years of Drumcree are simply a manifestation of two divided peoples, and that is the root of the problem. It's not just a marching issue. It's two opposing ways of life".[8]

---

6   The Times 12 July 1995
7   Sunday Independent 27 April 1997
8   Portadown Times 20 March 2001

Paul Dixon, a political analyst, very aptly commented, "The conflict over Drumcree represented an alternative indicator of public opinion to elections and opinion polls".[9]

As the protest at Drumcree gathered momentum, I realised that this "Battle of Ulster", as it was called, a battle for civil freedom is what made Drumcree significant for the whole of Northern Ireland and aroused so much media attention internationally.

The anomalous situation cannot remain in Northern Ireland, of on one hand the Assembly working for differences to be agreed and divisions to be healed, and on the other hand a visible manifestation of difference and division continuing at Drumcree and on the Garvaghy Road.

The truth is that without the 1998 parade at Drumcree being completed by proceeding along the Garvaghy Road to Portadown, the Orange Order will feel its parading rights are thwarted and unionists as a whole will feel their identity and culture is in jeopardy.

It will only be after such a parade that the Orange Order and the unionist population will feel secure for the foreseeable future. This means that the nationalists will also feel more secure.

---

9   Paul Dixon, "Northern Ireland", (Palgrave 2001) p263

Chapter 19
Drumcree and Religious Freedom

FOR me the issue of religious freedom became the
sensitive issue which exercised me most of all and with
which I had to deal personally and in a determined
manner.

During the years of crisis at Drumcree I had to endure
continually receiving messages spoken and written,
prevailing upon me to refuse members of the Orange
Order their right of public worship of Almighty God at
Drumcree in July. These messages came from individuals
and groups such as the 160 clergy in a petition in 1998, the
General Synod Motion in 1999, and the threat of new

legislation in the Church of Ireland to take away *my* freedom to have an open door church policy. I had to deal politely, but firmly, with all that was said to me and insist clearly and emphatically that I rejected all those messages, declaring unequivocally that I would never deny the right of worship to anyone, Orangemen or anyone else.

Orangemen come to worship on the first Sunday in July every year, like everyone else who attends on any Sunday throughout the year. In fact many regular worshippers are Orangemen, who are devoted completely to the Church of Ireland and the Orange Order. It would have been absolutely absurd for me at any time to turn away a worshipper because he was wearing a sash. It would be against all the principles of our country's cherished religious freedom to turn anyone away from worship. I often think of an individual worshipper coming to Drumcree Church every Sunday. His name could, for example be Billy and I would always welcome him. Then on the first Sunday in July Billy comes in a parade, with a sash around his neck. It would be beyond reason for me to say to him, "Billy, you cannot enter the church today." As far as I am concerned people may come to church *if* they wish, *when* they wish and *however* they wish, by walking, by parading, by car, by bicycle, by motorcycle, by tractor, by canoe or by helicopter. Those people who think that the Orange Order should stop parading to church, are not being realistic.

Attendance at church is a human right for everyone. The "Human Rights Act" 1998 Article 9. 1 'Freedom of thought, conscience and religion' says, "Everyone has the right to freedom of thought, conscience and religion or belief and freedom, either alone or in community with others and in public or private, to manifest his religion or belief, in worship, teaching, practice and observation".

But above that, attendance at church is a God given right for everyone. The Church of Ireland, throughout history, has had a free access policy, as is the case with all the churches, Reformed, Roman Catholic and Orthodox. Jesus said, "My house shall be a house of prayer for all nations." Mark 11:17 (Isaiah 56:7). This verse also says, "But you have made it a den of thieves." The religious rulers of the Temple at Jerusalem were robbing the Gentiles of their right to worship, in denying them space in their court, by allowing it to be filled with trading stalls. I saw the General Synod of 1999 as being akin to a den of robbers, robbing Orangemen of their right to worship at Drumcree. Why was the Church of Ireland so particular about who should enter its church buildings, and yet neglect to show love to all people.

When I reflect upon my ordination vows I am so aware that they included an obligation to bring people into services of worship to hear the gospel. For me to prevent people worshipping God, would be a complete denial of what my ordination meant to me.

And it is important that people come to church to discover that they are sinners and need to obtain pardon and new life by repentance of sin and faith in Christ who died on the cross to be their Saviour.

After everything the General Synod said about Drumcree it is interesting, that in the 2007 Church of Ireland Service of Institution of an incumbent (rector) the bishop presents him with the key of the church and says, "... let the doors of this place be open to all people."

It is ironic that these words were said to the new Rector of Drumcree, Rev. Gary Galway at his Institution on Wednesday 4th September 2008 by Archbishop Alan Harper , who when he was Archdeacon of Connor was the proposer of the 1999 General Synod Motion which called for Orangemen to be barred from attending worship at Drumcree Church.

I believe that the question of religious freedom was the most important matter that I dealt with at Drumcree, as I assured the members of the Orange Order and everyone else, that I would always welcome them to the public worship of Almighty God.

In my retirement, as I look back and think of how the Church of Ireland wanted me to close my church door and distance myself from the dispute at Drumcree, now I am interested to hear that the Hard Gospel Project of the Church of Ireland has concluded that Drumcree brought the Church of Ireland to deal with sectarianism.

Yet it seems to have been unnoticed that it was sectaranism I was trying to deal with from 1995. And I believe that without my efforts there could have been disaster for Drumcree and the Church of Ireland.

Chapter 20
Drumcree and the Church of Ireland

I believe that Drumcree is seen as the place where the Church of Ireland, which has always been known as an all-Ireland Protestant Church, continues to be defined by northern churchmen generally as Protestant, while being defined by southern churchmen as generally ecumenical.

From the Reformation in 1536, through the Disestablishment of 1871 and into the early part of the twentieth century, although the Church of Ireland in the south was not a majority church, it was very influential throughout the country in the professions and in business.

Unfortunately throughout those years the church's numbers suffered depletion at various times, such as the 1641 Rebellion, when many were murdered, the 1840 Potato Famine when many died and many more emigrated to America, the 1908 Ne Temere decree when many contracted marriages with Roman Catholics and after the Declaration of Independence in 1916 and partition in 1921, by emigration to Northern Ireland and England.

As the south came increasingly to be seen as a Catholic country for a Catholic people with the Roman Catholic Church wielding more and more power which is well described by Paul Blanchford[1] the Church of Ireland, as Patsy McGarry says, "adopted a low profile and maintained a separateness from the Roman Catholic Church and the State, who did little to help the Church of Ireland draw closer."[2]

When I was appointed to Ballinamore Parish in County Leitrim in 1967 I was told that up to the mid 1960s at Church of Ireland funeral services, Roman Catholics, who wished to attend, were not permitted to enter any of its churches, and at the graveside they were required to keep at a distance from the Church of Ireland mourners, the grass area between them being very evident.   Indeed, when the Protestant President Douglas Hyde[3] died in 1949 Roman Catholic Cabinet

1   "The Irish and Catholic Power" (1954)
2   Irish Times 12th May 1988
3   R. F. Foster, "Luck and the Irish" (Allen Lane, 2007) p.56

ministers were not allowed to enter church for his funeral service.

As the 1960's progressed, a new liberal era began, with easier access to education, more availability for travel, the growth of the media and the holding of the Second Vatican Council, which resulted in the Church of Ireland and the Roman Catholic Church drawing closer to each other. All of this has its positive aspects. I believe that where there can be co-operation it is right that it should take place, but where there can be no co-operation the churches need to be able to agree to differ while maintaining friendliness.

However, in the midst of these developments there were those in the Church of Ireland in the north, who began to draw apart, to a certain degree, from many parts of the church in the south. This happened because there were those in the church in the north who saw a liberalism in the church in the south meeting with a liberalism in the Roman Catholic Church there, allowing for common ground to be developed between the two churches and leading to an ecumenism, which they regard as unscriptural and not in accordance with the history of the Church of Ireland.

It needs to be remembered that the position of the Church of Ireland from the Reformation is set forth in the Preamble and Declaration of 1870, which may be found in the Book of Common Prayer 2004 page 776. I quote Section One:

"The Church of Ireland as a reformed and

Protestant Church, doth hereby re-affirm its constant witness against all those innovations in doctrine and worship, whereby the Primitive Faith hath been from time to time defaced and overlaid, and which at the Reformation this Church did disown and reject."

The churchmen in the north, who were uncomfortable with the ecumenism that they were seeing, regarded it as bringing the Church of Ireland, in the south in particular, to be something less than a distinctive Protestant Church. They were justified in these feelings when Motion Two was passed at the General Synod in 1999, stating, "...negative statements towards the Christians should not be seen as representing the spirit of the Church today." Their feelings are borne out by the Church of Ireland Standing Committee Report 1999, page 183, where it says in section A 3.31 "the church has changed".

"Since the sixteenth century Reformation, the Church of Ireland, with most of the Christian Churches, has changed and has gained new insights into the Christian faith."

So when members of the Orange Order, which was set up *"to support and defend the Protestant religion,"*[4] attend services in Church of Ireland churches, including

---

4 What is the Orange Order? (1997)

Drumcree, it goes against the grain of many southern churchmen, who are ecumenically minded.

However, when the General Synod of 1999 attempted to deny Orangemen the right to worship in Drumcree, but failed to do so, in spite of what may be said about the Church of Ireland being ecumenical in the south, I believe that the Protestantism of the Church of Ireland was strongly affirmed in a symbolic way at Drumcree in July 1999.

Despite many attempts by the General Synod throughout these years to undermine Drumcree's stance for religious and civil freedom, common sense has prevailed, and the Church of the Ascension at Drumcree quietly continues to pursue its future, guided by the principles set out in the Bible and the Prayer Book for all to read.

Chapter 21

Drumcree and the Media

THE media, - visual, audio and written - dictates what the world hears about a given situation. Their 'angle' influences the general public's view of a situation, and so it was with Drumcree.

The massive attention of the media, especially in the early years, completely overwhelmed me. I was not trained for dealing with the media. I had no experience of it and so I was completely unprepared to be involved in what was an unknown world for me. I was very timid at the beginning, nearly standing at the wrong side of a camera at times, or almost freezing before a microphone thrust in front of me, at other times.

My first encounter with the media began because the LOL, unwisely, were not speaking to the media, and anyway, they did not have any representatives to do so. As all media interviews at Drumcree were coming from the GRRC viewpoint, I decided that I should explain what was happening on the Hill, trying to make clear that, while I supported the Orange's right to march, Drumcree Parish itself was not directly involved.   Later, the LOL rectified their omission and appointed David Jones as their media representative.

First live TV interview   *Olive Pickering*

I soon learnt that the three branches in the media - television, radio, and newspaper, with their presenters, reporters and journalists, all used different styles along with their own individual methods of dealing with events.

Because I was mostly on news broadcasts, I saw that I was required to use the 'sound bite' approach, so I had to decide on the few words that I wanted to convey. If I was being interviewed on live television or radio, then I could get my words across very easily. However, if it was a recorded interview, I repeated the 'sound bite' several times at the same interview, to the point of embarrassment, to try to ensure my words would be broadcast, in case the producer or editor decided to use only a small portion of what I had said.

I did not often give lengthy interviews for television or radio, or for current affairs style programmes or newspaper feature articles. For these interviews I had to use a different style, which amounted to giving much more detailed answers.

The media has its own way of showing 'news'. I came to understand that I should always say what *I* wanted to say, no matter what the question was that I was being asked, perhaps a bit like a politician. This approach I found strange, because I had been taught to give a straight and helpful answer to any question that I was asked. But this is not so in dealing with the media. I learnt to say to myself that the viewers and hearers should be more interested in the point I wished to get across, than to listen to the question from the interviewer. How else would my viewpoint get a hearing!

The vast number of media people who came to Drumcree from all over the world was unbelievable. The attention that they gave to the Drumcree situation was staggering. The church on the Hill was shown, day and night, as the background to practically every interview given.

In 1995, 1996 and 1997 the media took up position on the security force side of the barrier, with their TV camera crews, photographers, radio interviewers with their tape recorders, along with newspaper reporters and their notebooks. A long row of outside broadcast vehicles with satellite dishes lined the side of the road. Uplifts were used for better filming. Then from 1998 the media also came to the "Orange" side, and at times the road was thick with them, as they showed at least some of the activity there. Some would say often they showed only the unruly elements, rather than the community spirit which, on the whole, prevailed.

The media people of the British Isles whom I met represented BBC1, BBC NI, BBC2, BBC 24, BBC World Service, UTV, ITV, RTE, TNAG, SKY, TV3, CH4, Euro News, ITN, APTN, Cool FM, Downtown Radio, Radio Craigavon, UCB, Premier Radio, Radio Luton, City Beat; Portadown Times, Ulster Gazette, News Letter, Belfast Telegraph, Irish News, Sunday Life, Irish Times, Irish Independent, The Times, Evening Herald, The Scotsman, The Herald, Independent, Guardian, Daily Mail, Daily Express, Daily Record, Mirror, Reuters, PA and AP. Thankfully, not all at once!

The media from Europe with whom I had interviews represented countries including France, Germany, Spain, Sweden, Italy, Holland, Finland, Denmark, Hungary and

Russia. In North America, the media, with whom I had contact, were represented mainly by CBS, CBC, CNN, New York Times, Herald Tribune, Boston Herald, Toronto Star and National Post. I trust they used the information I gave them fairly and wisely.

Some interviews were pre-arranged by a phone call or a visit, but most were spontaneous over the phone, or on location, usually at Drumcree Church or rectory, pre-recorded or live. On certain occasions I issued to the media faxed 'news items', otherwise known as 'press releases', when I wished to make certain information available to the general public. Sometimes I provided the media with printed statements, as I met them. At particular times I would invite the media to the Rectory for a 'press briefing', quite like a 'press conference' if there was a matter of importance with which to be dealt.

From the early days of Drumcree I was much aware of the advantages of being involved with the media. The methods used are *'fast'* and so I was able to get my message across immediately, as in the live interview, or very soon on the next news bulletin, or within twenty-four hours in the case of newspapers. The media communications are *'far-reaching'*, going all over the world. One morning I spoke live on BBC TV World Service to an audience of forty-six million people. And of course, the coverage I was getting by the media was *'free'*!

There were amusing episodes, such as when a drunken man almost stumbled in between a camera man and me, on which occasion an army Colonel, who was standing nearby, came to the rescue.

I am pleased to say that I was treated with utmost courtesy and kindness, often being allowed to re-start an interview several times for the sake of clarity, 'a privilege not allowed to politicians', as I was told by the interviewers. I was always represented very fairly. Of course there were a few exceptions, such as when loaded questions were asked, which demanded a yes or no answer, which could lead to a blind alley. So my response to that style of question was to say: "I thought that you would know the answer". I am indebted to my lawyer friend, Richard Monteith, for that piece of advice.

However, I am pleased that I came to know a good number of the members of the media, and my friendship with them has remained strong and is always much valued.

In the early years I had the helpful assistance of the Church of Ireland Press Officer, Mrs Elizabeth Gibson-Harries. Later I had Parish Press Officers: Kathryn Anderson, Jenna Rankin and Beryl Robinson, which proved very helpful.

I did not choose to have such a public role in a highly topical situation, rather it was thrust upon me, given the dramatic events which developed at my church, so I had to deal with what arose as it occurred. As I have discovered, there are many advantages, but also disadvantages, to being continually in the news!

Chapter 22
Drumcree and My Role

I often wonder how I happened to be the Rector of Drumcree at such an extremely difficult time. I did not have any background experience to help me to handle this serious situation. I felt that I was plunged so deeply and so quickly into a completely new experience along with Olive and Sarah. The nature of the situation was such that a number of complex issues were happening at the same time and it was most difficult to cope with everything that was going on.

In the early years the **large crowd** of people who came every day was unbelievable, for what was a quiet country area in County Armagh. What a sight it was to see lodges and bands who came from all parts of the province in thousands. They parked their cars and buses for great distances along the roadsides and in the fields, including the rectory field which was filled every day, especially in the evenings of July 1998.

Immediately after arriving everyone headed to the bridge and joined the assembled crowd. As the crowd grew it spread into the field along by the stream alongside the army razor wire fence. It became quite impossible to walk on the roads at times, so I had to resort to being re-routed across the fields!

The **noise** which kept coming from the chattering of the people, the music of bands, the explosions of the fireworks, the bangs of the plastic bullets, the sound of helicopters overhead and the landing of soldiers in the fields around the rectory was quite an experience for this area. Then the infiltration of troublemakers, over which there was no control, was very alarming, most unnerving and such a serious threat to life and limb. Unfortunately some people were badly injured. Olive and I felt so helpless as we observed these events.

The constant ringing of the **telephone** was something new to me. Olive was of great assistance in dealing with the huge volume of calls. It was always a great pleasure and delight to receive so many calls from people giving assurance of their good wishes and prayers. Many of the callers phoned with advice for a resolution to the crisis, but there were a number of nuisance calls too.

At times Drumcree took some toll on my **health**. It affected my natural pattern of eating and sleeping properly and Olive was affected similarly. I am not suggesting that Olive and I were the only ones disturbed because so many people have suffered so dreadfully in so many places and for very long periods, but I am recording the effect the troubles at Drumcree had on Olive and me.

Being placed in this situation, through no fault of my own, I asked myself what positive attitude I should take towards it. Faced with such a difficult and perplexing situation I could have easily decided to go away immediately after the Orange Service. I could have gone away on a holiday. Or, as time progressed and the situation became more complicated and stressful, I could have left the parish altogether and sought ministry elsewhere. However, that would have been absolutely wrong to do, because it would mean I would have been abrogating my responsibilities to God, who had called me to the parish.

So I decided to stay at Drumcree. I realised that the people at Drumcree were in great distress and needed me, the rector, to help them. I saw that the Orange Order was feeling it did not have a friend, so I decided to be that friend. During my ministry I have always understood that I should be a friend to those in need, to help them in their plight, and this was a time to bring the practical assistance required. I am well aware that many criticisms have been made about the Orange Order, concerning their lack of discipline at times and this I would often have concurred with, but when I saw the Order in need, that was a much different matter and it required a pro-active approach.

I reflected upon the fact that the Lord Jesus Christ became incarnate and entered the world showing utmost understanding of the needs of all people and exercising absolute compassion towards them. As I thought of how Christ mixed among needy people and helped them, I took him as my example to do the best I could for the needy people at Drumcree. So it became obvious to me that I should seek to be God's man. I began to feel like the prophet Ezekiel, a man whom C. G. Howie[1] describes as, "a sensitive human soul caught in the crosscurrents of history, driven by a burning zeal for God, painfully aware of the tragedy in which his people were involved."

J. B. Taylor[2] described Ezekiel as, "a man who, combined in a unique way, the priest's sense of the holiness of God, the prophet's sense of the message that had been entrusted to him and the pastor's sense of responsibility for his people." While recognising, of course, what an absolutely pale reflection I am of Ezekiel, nevertheless I have been considerably strengthened by that great prophet.

I sought to be a **priest** at all times, praying and encouraging others to do likewise, at home, at church services and at prayer meetings, of which many were held at Drumcree.

---

1   C. G. Howie "Ezekiel, Daniel" (1961) p15
2   J. B. Taylor, "Ezekiel (IVP 1969) (I am indebted to the author for personally introducing his book to me in 1980)

In seeking to be a **prophet** I simply did my best to bring the Word of God to the people directly from the Holy Scriptures.[3] While I never believed there would be any great voice speaking from heaven, I always believed that it would be that "still, small voice"[4] that would bring the message needed. All the time I was determined to show that there is always hope, in even the most apparently hopeless situations, illness, bereavement, guilt, and that God is a God of hope, who can make "dry bones live." (Ezekiel 37:5) All along I stressed the importance of faith in God through the Lord Jesus Christ which required definite commitment.

I sought at all times to be a **peacemaker** and keep calm, assuring others that this was the only attitude to have in any crisis. On occasions, by the use of a powerful loudspeaker, I had some success in quieting the unruly element. An example of this occurred on Monday 8th July 1996 at 3.00pm when the security forces moved the Orangemen on the Hill at Drumcree, the crowd became very agitated, and David Trimble remonstrated with the RUC in the churchyard. When I telephoned the 'control room,' the RUC assured me that the army was simply strengthening the defences at the bridge and needed the crowd moved to do so. I am glad that when I spoke to the crowd they settled and calm was restored immediately. At this time, unknown to me, Brownstown Road was being blocked and vehicles were being burned, but

---

3   Psalms 46 and 59 were two of these passages.
4   1 Kings 19:12

after my announcement the burning of vehicles ceased too.

On another occasion I had to rebuke a young man for directing a laser pen towards the police. Twelve months afterwards he came to me and said, "I was so ashamed of myself that I decided to change my way of life and become a Christian".

On Sunday 4th July 1999 the effect of the Orangemen going to the rectory field for a briefing, at my behest, had a profound calming influence for that day and some time following.

And of course I worked tirelessly for a resolution to the crisis by talking to the Parades Commission, the Police the Orange Order and politicians. I wish that I had been able to do more.

In this complex and difficult situation I came to see myself as a pastor to the people at Drumcree. I trust that I was a helpful **pastor**, listening carefully to the anxieties of the people and seeking to assist them with my advice in their hour of need. As I moved among the people continually I believe I was not seen to be the pastor leaving the sheep without a shepherd, and so I believe I perhaps brought some strength to them.

The Drumcree situation was the ultimate challenge for any minister, as it called for someone to maintain the normal church activities amid a very abnormal series of events. I trust I carried this out as God would have intended.

Appendices

APPENDIX A

SERMON – PSALM 59

Preached at the Cathedral of the Advent Birmingham, Alabama on Sunday 28 March 2004. This sermon was a development of one I had preached at Drumcree Parish Church on Sunday 28 June 1998. I am indebted to the unknown source which provided the basis of this sermon.

I am sure that you often feel like me when you find yourself in the middle of an impossible situation or almost impossible situation. You try as hard as you can to find a solution, but nothing seems to help.

I have found this in my Parish of Drumcree near Portadown in Northern Ireland, where since July 1995 the residents of Garvaghy Road object to the members of the Protestant Orange Order walking along that road on their return to Portadown after attending morning service at Drumcree Church on the first Sunday in July every year. The residents object because they say the road is inhabited by Roman Catholic people. The Orange Order says that they are simply returning from church as they have been doing by tradition since 1807, and the road is a main road. The residents want to talk with the Orange Order before a walk. The Orange Order wants to walk first and then talk about future parades. It has been described as an impossible situation.

But I have learned from the Scriptures that we need a Biblical perspective on this impossible situation. And I have learned how much we need a Biblical perspective on any impossible situation.

Back in 1998 my attention was drawn to one of the places in the Bible where it is shown that there is help in impossible situations. And that place was Psalm 59. I saw there that the writer David was in serious trouble. I looked at his reaction. And I learned from him. And I believe that no matter in what impossible situation we may find ourselves in Northern Ireland, the United States of America or anywhere else, Psalm 59 gives us help. This Psalm tells us:

(a) GOD SEES

God saw the plight of David. Verse 3 *"See how they lie in wait for me"* ie God sees you and God knows about you. David was oppressed by something. What the problem was we are not sure. He could have been troubled because Saul had sent men out to kill him or from his regret at yielding to temptation over Bathsheba. He was surrounded by something awful, he was intimidated by it, he was nearly overcome by it. Verses 1 and 2 *"Deliver me from my enemies, O God; protect me from those who rise up against me. Deliver me from evildoers and save me from bloodthirsty men."*

People often feel like that today because of suffering illness, bereavement, loneliness, unkindness from a neighbour, guilt or some other need.

But remember, as God saw David, he also sees you in your plight and he knows all about your difficulties and your need for help. And God has sympathy for you. Jesus wept at the grave of Lazarus and he wept over Jerusalem. He understands your plight.

So when you realise that God sees you in your plight, what do you do?

You pray to God. God saw David's difficulties, He knew all about them. So David realised he should pray to God, talk to God about his problems.Verses 3, 4 and 5a "O Lord I have done no wrong, yet they are ready to attack me. Arise to help me; look on my plight! O Lord God Almighty, the God of Israel." So God is teaching us here to pray to him about our needs. James 4 : 2 says "You do not have because you do not ask God". Ezekiel 36:37 "This is what the Sovereign Lord says, Once again I will yield to the plea of the house of Israel".

Back in my parish, God was nearby during the most difficult summers with much violence. I believe that matters would have been much worse and someone might even have been killed, except for the fact that we prayed. And we prayed in 2003 for peace in July and there was peace. It was the best summer since before 1995.

And of course your worst problem is that you are a sinner and your sin will keep you out of heaven unless you repent. God sees your plight. So what do you do?

You must pray the sinner's prayer, "God be merciful to me a sinner".

(b) GOD HEARS

God heard the cry of David. David's enemies did not think anyone was hearing the cry of David in his affliction. His enemies asked, *"Who can hear us?"* in verse 7b. But they did not know that God heard. And God heard the cries of David suffering affliction. God was listening to David. David's enemies were like snarling dogs. Verse 6 and 7a *"They return at evening, snarling like dogs, and prowl about the city. See what they spew from their mouths"*. They came in the evening or the night-time when David was at his weakest. His enemies attack could well have been an attack of depression. The reference to dogs could point to black dog, which is a common everyday way of describing depression. That is how Sir Winston Churchill described his depression.

Many people are depressed by many things such as problems in their family, their country and the world. Many people are depressed by the guilt of their sins. But remember, as God heard the cry of David, so He hears your cry also.

And when you realise that God hears you what do you do?

You wait on God. Verse 9 *"O my Strength, I watch (or I wait) for you"*. Very often you just have to be patient and wait for God to help you in his own time and his own way. Waiting is part of life. You have to wait for examination results, the results of an election, to get a job, to purchase a property, get married, for the birth of a child, to receive results of a medical test, and so on.

At Drumcree one July morning at 4.30am, I received a phone call to say that there had been some damage done to a number of headstones in the churchyard. It was still dark and I could not see what had happened. I had to wait until daylight. Thankfully no damage had been done, but I had to wait to find out. God hears your cry; just wait on him for help. Whatever your need is, be it of body or soul, just wait on God. Isaiah 40 : 31 says, "... they who wait for the Lord shall renew their strength, they shall mount up with wings of eagles, they shall run and not be weary, they shall walk and not faint". Psalm 46 : 10 says, "Be still and know that I am God".

(c) GOD RULES

In verses 10 – 13 David says that he knows God will deal with his enemies because God is the ruler. Verse 13 emphasised that God rules. It says *"God rules over Jacob"*. It also says Selah, which means, take good note of that.

David has utter confidence in God that He would stop his enemies in their attacks upon him. And David is certain that the people will know it. He says in verse 13, *"Then it will be known to the ends of the earth"*. Be confident that God rules, he is the Sovereign Lord in your life. He is in control. He may seem far away, but he is not absent. When you realise that God rules, what do you do? **You trust in him**.

David says in verse 11, *"O Lord our shield"*. David was saying that God was his shield and he knew he could trust him. David had every confidence in God that he would reign over him and rescue him.

It can be so easy for us to get overwhelmed by our problems and get down under them. But we must not be like that, because God is the Lord of all, he is the Sovereign Lord, he is in control. He holds the whole world in the hollow of his hand.

When the General Synod of the Church of Ireland passed a motion seeking to prevent members of the Orange Order from attending worship at Drumcree, I believe God ruled in the situation. I believe that he overruled. I believe that in due course people came to see that attendance at worship was a God-given right, a God-ordained right. People came to see that if the church door had been closed the trouble would have escalated. And certainly last summer, which was quiet, there would have been no peace if the door had been closed. As we accept God's rule we learn to trust Him and experience his fulfilment in our lives.

(d) GOD DELIVERS

Even though the going was very hard for David he knew God would deliver him. The going was really very hard. Verse 14 and 15 *"They return at evening, snarling like dogs, and prowl about the city. They wander about for food and howl if not satisfied"*. But David was able to say, Verse 16b and 17b *"For you are my fortress, my refuge in times of trouble", and ," O God, you are my fortress, my loving God"*.

You too should realise that God delivers. What do you do?

You hope in God. What was David doing here when he said he knew God would deliver Him?   He was expressing hope.   He said, *"I will sing"* three times in verses 16 and 17 *"But I will sing of your strength"*, *"in the morning I will sing of your love"* and *"O my Strength, I sing praise to you"*.

And God will deliver you from your need. There is hope for you whatever your need. Isaiah 40 : 31 "... those who hope in the Lord will renew their strength". There is hope because of the resurrection of the Lord Jesus Christ. Christ is alive today and so you may be filled with all hope through believing in Him. There is hope for your bodily material, mental and spiritual needs. There is hope for the Church, for each of our countries, the Anglican Communion and evangelicalism in the whole world, in Christ.

God can do the unexpected thing. He did it at the first Easter. And I believe God will do the unexpected thing again for our need whatever it may be.

I have always spoken to reporters about hope in our situation at Drumcree. I remember well speaking about hope to them on Sunday evening 6 July 1997, about change that could come in due course. Five days later, in a surprise move, the Orange Order announced that four controversial parades would be re-routed on 12th July. Also the IRA surprisingly announced a ceasefire. And so I was vindicated in what I had said about hope being real.

When you hope for God to deliver you from your sins and give you eternal life, you know most assuredly that he will fulfil his promise of salvation. Jesus said, "I give them eternal life and they shall never perish, and no-one can snatch them out of my hand" John 10 : 28.

So no matter in what difficult situation you may find yourself, be encouraged by Psalm 59, which David wrote when he was in trouble. Remember: God sees you in your time of trouble, so pray to him; God hears you, so wait on him; God rules, so just trust him and God delivers, so be filled with hope in him.

This is true for my situation, for your situation, for the needs of body and soul, for now and forever.

Drumcree Church   *John Pickering*

APPENDIX B

NEWS ITEMS

EMBARGO – MONDAY 12th OCTOBER 1998 7.00pm
ORANGEMEN ATTENDING DRUMCREE

The call to prevent Orangemen attending Morning Prayer in Drumcree Parish Church in July every year has been rejected by the Rector the Rev John Pickering and his Select Vestry. The call came from a Church of Ireland Group of 160 ordained clergy.

Mr Pickering says that he is very sorry the group seems not to understand the situation at Drumcree, and regrets they did not consult with him before issuing their letter which was sent to all ordained clergy of the Church of Ireland. While the clergy received their letters in August, Mr Pickering does not understand why he did not receive his until October.

Mr Pickering says "It must be stressed that nobody can be denied the right to a service to worship Almighty God." He says, "I want to state clearly that I will never deny the right of worship to any person, including any member of the Orange Order. Let there be no doubt that Morning Prayer will be held on the Sunday before 12 July every year as it is held every Sunday."

Mr Pickering observes, "I am interested that 680 ordained clergy, approx, did not sign the letter, from which it may be assumed they have an understanding of Drumcree and perhaps reject the call in the letter."

From: Rev John Pickering, 78 Drumcree Road, Portadown.

Irish News, 21 October 1998

DRUMCREE PARISH CHURCH – SUNDAY 4 JULY 1999 11.30am

SUMMARY OF THE SERMON PREACHED BY THE REV JOHN PICKERING

The rolls of razor wire I see stretched along the fields across from the church and the metal barrier on the road is again this year a symbol of the sad divisions in Northern Ireland.

The saddest division this morning is the division there is between people and God. However relationship with God may be restored by faith in the Lord Jesus Christ. If people have that vertical relationship with God, then they will have a horizontal relationship with each other.

God is the only One who can heal our divisions and bring us peace and hope forever.

Rev John Pickering, Drumcree Rectory, 78 Drumcree Road, Portadown BT62 1PE.

DRUMCREE PARISH CHURCH SUNDAY 9th JULY 2000 11.30AM

SUMMARY OF THE SERMON PREACHED BY THE REV JOHN PICKERING

The bridge, the stream and the razor wire fence in the valley beyond Drumcree Church maybe seen as a symbol of a valley of heaviness of heart about many things including the situation at Drumcree today. The barrier speaks of division and separation and of an end.

But the Church of Drumcree at the top of the hill should be a symbol of uplift for it points to God and witnesses to hope.

When David in the Old Testament was in despair he wrote, "I

will lift up mine eyes unto the hills, from whence comes my help. My help comes from the Lord who made heaven and earth." Psalm 121 vs 1 & 2

DRUMCREE PARISH CHURCH - SUNDAY 8 JULY 2001

SUMMARY OF THE SERMON BY REV JOHN PICKERING

The barrier on the road at the bridge beyond the church seems to many people to be saying in a very visual manner that this is the end of the road for the Orangemen and the end of the road for Northern Ireland.

But this barrier need not be saying we are at any end in the life of our country. There is life and hope for all of us in the area and this country. This hope is by trust in the Lord Jesus Christ who can give us the right relationship with God and our fellow man and time for peace and stability for the days to come and forever.

From The Rev John Pickering, Rector of Drumcree

DRUMCREE PARISH   PETITION TO THE
ARCHBISHOP
OPEN CHURCH DOOR   NO SERVICES TO BE
CANCELLED

At this month's meeting of the Select Vestry of Drumcree Parish held on Wednesday, 9 October 2002, it was confirmed that Drumcree parishioners had signed and delivered a Petition to the Archbishop of Armagh, The Most Rev'd Dr RHA Eames.

The Petition was in support of the principled stand of the rector, Rev John A Pickering, in his open church door policy for everyone.

Also the Petition supported the importance of resisting any change to the laws of the Church of Ireland, whereby a Bishop would be given authority to cancel church services.

Drumcree Parish is not in dispute with the Archbishop. The Petition was given to the Archbishop simply because he is Primate of the Church of Ireland.

From Drumcree Parish Select Vestry

13 October 2002

NEWSPAPER REPRODUCTIONS

THE IRISH TIMES

August 6th, 1996
Letters to the Editor

AFTER DRUMCREE

Sir, - I refer to the Very Rev. Victor G. Griffin's letter of July 31st. How easy it is for the retired Dean of St Patrick's Cathedral, Dublin, to write from his armchair in Limavady and to criticize the clergy after the events at Drumcree. If the Dean feels he could have resolved the problem, why did he not come to Drumcree? His presence and advice would have been most welcome.

To make public comments on the events which he only watched on his TV screen, and never experienced through his many years of ministry in Northern Ireland and the Irish Republic, does nothing to help and encourage those clergy who worked long hours before and during the crisis, trying to bring it to a peaceful end.

Yours etc,. OLIVE PICKERING, The Rectory, Drumcree Road, Portadown BT62 1PE.

News Letter
First published in 1737

MORNING VIEW

Saturday, July 8, 2006

DRUMCREE REMAINS IN PROTRACTED DEADLOCK

The annual Drumcree Orange parade in Portadown takes place tomorrow and once again lodge members are prevented from parading back from a church service along their traditional Garvaghy Road route which dates back nearly 200 years.

The Parades Commission, not surprisingly has ruled that the Garvaghy Road is out of bounds for the marchers and a stand-off will continue for at least another year, barring an unlikely agreement being worked out between the Orange Order and nationalist residents.

Portadown Orangemen and women who parade to morning worship tomorrow will do so peacefully and with dignity.

Drumcree rector the Rev John Pickering alluded to a possible template for progress when, ahead of tomorrow's service, he said; "The real issue is one of identity, and we need to work to create a situation where each side can respect the other's identity and no longer feel threatened."

No-one has been closer to the Drumcree stand-off for the past 12 years than Mr Pickering and, from his own particular perspective on the controversy that has surrounded his parish, he does deserve to be listened to.

Wednesday, October 21, 1998
DOING THINGS THE HARD WAY

One of the golden rules about the complexity of Northern Ireland is this; beware of simple solutions. Therefore, anyone who believes that the simple solution to the Drumcree mess is to pressurize the local vicar to close his doors to the local Orangemen, needs to think again.

The Rev John Pickering is a decent man trapped in an impossible situation. For years he and the Orange Order hierarchy have shown not only do they have no control over events, but that they are powerless to stop the Drumcree demonstration in the first place.

And if Mr Pickering did close his church, the brethren would simply hold a drumhead service outside.

No matter how one might wish the Drumcree debacle to be solved, the simple answer is not to ban the Orangemen, or anyone else, from worship.

Whatever the pressures, Mr Pickering should hold his ground and keep his church open to all.

THE IRISH TIMES

Wednesday 14 October 1998

By Suzanne Breen, in Belfast

The Democratic Unionist Party has strongly supported the rector of Drumcree parish church, the Rev John Pickering, who has rejected calls to prevent Orangemen attending their annual service there next July.

Mr Pickering recently received a letter signed by 160 Church of Ireland clergy asking him not to allow the Order to use his church.

The letter was sent by the ecumenical Church of Ireland group, Catalyst.

The DUP leader, the Rev Ian Paisley, said Mr Pickering must be congratulated for his principled stand. "No man has the right to call for a church to be closed. It is a sign of just how far the authorities would go to silence Protestantism and rob us of our very right to worship. Well done, Rev Pickering. You are an inspiration to those who believe in the doctrines of the Reformed faith and in freedom of worship."

News Letter
First published in 1737

MORNING VIEW

Wednesday, October 14, 1998

MINISTER RIGHT TO WELCOME ORDER

The Rev John Pickering has found himself in the middle of a holy row not of his own making. By refusing to ban Orangemen from the Somme Commemoration service in July, he has invoked the ire of the Church of Ireland hierarchy, including the Catalyst group which apparently wants all Orangemen to join the Free Presbyterian Church.

There are many grey issues surrounding Drumcree and the Garvaghy Road dispute, but in this instance there is only black and white, right and wrong.

The plain fact is that the Rev Pickering is right and those who have criticized him are not.

The Church of Ireland prides itself on being an ecumenical, pluralist church. How can it possibly square these principles with attempting to exclude certain people – including many long-standing members of its Drumcree congregation – from worship?

If the teachings of Christ are applied to this dispute, the grounds for complaint would be even thinner.

Is not the act of worship a matter for the individual, to be undertaken solemnly and as a matter of conscience by those who choose their own free will to enter the House of God?

If the Church of Ireland embarked on a crusade to exclude everyone with dubious politics or doubtful motives, its membership would be dramatically reduced across the whole island. Which is not to say that those members of the Orange Order who attend the Drumcree service do not do so with honourable intentions, and in a spirit of respect for the institution of the church and the principles it stands for.

The stand taken by Catalyst is particularly regrettable, because it has made little effort to familiarize itself with the very real issues involved in the Garvaghy Road dispute.

Rev Pickering should stand his ground. His duty is to open the doors of his church on a Sunday morning to anyone who wishes to enter, and to preach the Gospel.

BELFAST TELEGRAPH,
FRIDAY, JULY 2, 1999

HOW DRUMCREE CAN BECOME A SYMBOL OF HOPE

I am just an ordinary Church of Ireland clergyman seeking to do an ordinary job, as Rector of Drumcree Parish.

When I came to Drumcree in 1983 I never dreamt that I would find myself in this situation which is a microcosm of Northern Ireland today.

I take Morning Service in Drumcree Parish every Sunday morning and on the Sunday morning before the Twelfth of July weekend every year the Orangemen of Portadown District attend by custom.

The service is normal Morning Service which anyone may attend like anyone else. Attendance is a God given right and it is a human right.

My situation at the moment is that I have just received a communication from the General Synod of the Church of Ireland in the name of its honorary secretaries – the Very Rev H Cassidy, Dean of Armagh, Rev Canon D Harman, Rector of Sandford, Dublin, Mr S Harper, of Kilkenny and Lady B Shiel, of Belfast.

The communication, in effect, is asking that Orangemen be prevented from attending next Sunday morning's service at Drumcree.

My reaction to the communication is to say simply that anyone who wishes to attend morning service at Drumcree next Sunday, July 4, at 11.30 may attend, members of the Orange Order and anyone else.

Unfortunately, because of the problems of violence at Drumcree in recent years, which I utterly condemn, Drumcree Church has been perceived as the symbol of something awful, but there is no reason why it cannot be the symbol of good.

When the Lord Jesus Christ died and was laid in the tomb, his disciples were very despondent, forlorn and regarded the tomb as a symbol of despair.

But on the third day after Christ's death, he rose from the death and his tomb became a symbol of new life and hope forever.

Drumcree can be the symbol of new life and hope.

It would be great if Drumcree could become the turning point for Northern Ireland and there is no reason why that should not happen, because God can do the unexpected thing. Nothing is impossible with God.

As the weekend approaches it is imperative for people to exercise restraint, keep calm and have nothing to do with violence.

Above all, pray for God's help and trust in him for stability, peace and real hope for the days to come in all Portadown and the whole country.

THE PARISH OF DRUMCREE

PETITION

We, the parishioners of Drumcree Parish, support fully our rector, Rev. John Pickering, in maintaining his principled and Christian position of keeping the church doors open to all who wish to worship God and hear the gospel preached at our church.

NAME *(Please Print)*	ADDRESS	SIGNATURE
J HILLIGAN	DUNGANNON R.D. CRAIGAVON	
Y COOKE	DUNGANNON Rd PORTADOWN	
E M COOKE	DUNGANNON Rd PORTADOWN	
M. TAYLOR	Drumgoose Rd.	
Freddie Hall	DRUMGOOSE ROAD	
JANET HALL	DRUMGOOSE ROAD	
M F ROBERTA HALL	DRUMGOOSE ROAD PORTADOWN.	
F. J. HALL	DRUMGOOSE ROAD PORTADOWN	
ALBERT TAYLOR	DRUMINALLY Rd PORTADOWN	
REA TAYLOR	DRUMINALLY ROAD PORTADOWN	

APPENDIX C

LODGES IN PORTADOWN DISTRICT LOL NO 1 BETWEEN 1795-2009

- **Breagh Leading Heroes** LOL 7
- **Star of Drumherrif** LOL 8
- **Earl of Beaconsfield Primrose League** LOL 9, Clounagh
- **Greenisland True Blues** LOL 10, Derrinraw
- **The Rising Sons of William**, Derrinraw, LOL13
- **Brackagh Golden Springs** LOL18
- **Ballyworkan Truth Defenders** LOL19
- **Erin's Royal Standard** LOL 20, Kilmagamish
- **Bocombra True Blues** LOL 22
- **Wingfeld Verner's Crimson Star** LOL 25
- **Churchview** LOL 26, Seagoe
- **Bible and Crown Defenders** LOL 31, Kilmoriarty
- **Prince of Wales** LOL 56
- **St. Aidan's True Blues** LOL 35, Kilmore
- **Bible and Crown Defenders** LOL 78, Derrycarne
- **Col. Saunderson** LOL 58
- **Herbert Whitten Memorial** LOL 40
- **Star of the North** LOL 80, Ballylisk
- **Derryhale** LOL 81
- **Rechabs** LOL 89
- **Johnston's Royal Standard** LOL 99
- **Sir Edward Wingfield Verner's True Blues**, Knocknamuckley LOL 107
- **King William's Defenders** LOL 127, Parkmount
- **Wesleyan Temperance** LOL 161
- **St. Saviour's True Blues** LOL 172, Clonroot
- **Rising Sons of Portadown** LOL 273

- **R J Magowan Memorial Temperance** LOL 322, Edenderry
- **Corcraine Purple Rocket** LOL 339
- **Derrykeevan Temperance** LOL 352
- **Drumnahuncheon Apprentice Boys** LOL 371
- **Battlehill** LOL 395
- **Harmony** LOL 500
- **Dr. Kane's Crimson Star** LOL 417
- **Portadown Ex-Servicemen's** LOL 608

GLOSSARY

ACACS	The Advisory Conciliation and Arbitration Service.
ACC	Assistant Chief Constable.
Anglo-Irish Agreement	It was made in 1985 and gave the Republic of Ireland a say in the affairs of Northern Ireland.
APTN	Associated Press Television News.
BA	Bachelor in Arts.
Battle of the Boyne	William of Orange defeated James II in 1690.
BBC	British Broadcasting Corporation.
Carleton Street	The street in Portadown where a large Orange Hall is situated.
CBC	Canadian Broadcasting Corporation.
CBS	Columbian Broadcasting Service.
CCTV	Closed circuit television.
CH4	An ITN TV channel.
Church of Ireland	The oldest Church in Ireland, Protestant, Episcopal, Anglican.
CNN	Cable Network News.
CRC	Community Relations Council.
Declaration of Independence	An Irish declaration or proclamation of intent in 1916.

Defenders	An eighteenth century Catholic defence group.
Downing Street Agreement	An intergovernmental strategy statement issued in 1993 by John Major PM and the Irish Premier Albert Reynolds.
DUP	Democratic Unionist Party, founded in 1971 by Rev Ian Paisley who led it until 2008. It claims to give strength to unionism.
Framework Document	It set out proposals in 1995 for the governance of Northern Ireland.
Free Presbyterian Church	It was founded in 1951 by Rev Ian Paisley who was Moderator until 2008. It has congregations across all of Northern Ireland as well as a presence in the Republic of Ireland and other countries.
General Synod	The governing body of the Church of Ireland.
GOLI	Grand Orange Lodge of Ireland.
Good Friday Agreement	On Good Friday 1998 it was proposed to set up a NI Power-sharing Assembly.
GRRC	Garvaghy Road Residents' Coalition. It was founded in 1995 to oppose Orange parades on the Garvaghy Road, Portadown.
Home Rule	It refers to the aspiration for Ireland to be ruled separately from Great Britain. Bills for such were read in Westminster from 1886 for some years.
Independence	It refers to the 26 counties of Ireland having their sovereign rule.

IRA	Irish Republican Army, now known as the Provisional IRA. A large Irish paramilitary organisation, now inactive.
ITN	Independent Television News.
ITV	Independent Television.
LOL	Loyal Orange Lodge, founded in 1795 to help defend Protestantism.
LVF	Loyalist Volunteer Force. It is a loyalist paramilitary group in which Billy Wright was very active.
MA	Master in Arts.
MLA	Member of the NI Legislative Assembly.
Nationalist	One who aspires to an all-Ireland government by peaceful means, hoping to include British people by consent.
Ne Temere Decree	A regulation of the Roman Catholic Church in 1908 which gives it advantages in mixed marriages.
NI	Northern Ireland, the six counties in the north of Ireland, part of the United Kingdom.
NIE	Northern Ireland Electricity.
N I Forum	A body appointed to promote and develop politics.
NIO	Northern Ireland Office set up by Westminster to rule NI directly after the collapse of the Stormont Parliament in 1972.
PA	Press Association.

Parades Commission	It was set up in 1997 to decide about parades.
Peep O' Day	An eighteenth century violent Protestant group which attacked at the break of day.
PM	Prime Minister.
Portadown 2000	A group set up for the rejuvenation of Portadown.
Prayer Book	The Church of Ireland service book.
Protestant	One who asserts the Holy Scriptures (The Bible) as the supreme authority for faith and morals, as established at the Reformation.
PSNI	Police Service Northern Ireland. After the Patten report, this title was given to a reformed RUC in Northern Ireland in November 2001.
QUB	Queen's University Belfast.
RCB	Representative Church Body. The Church of Ireland trustee body.
Reformation	A religious movement dated from 1517 when Martin Luther, a German Catholic priest, publicly protested against certain practices of the Roman Catholic Church.
Republic of Ireland	The 26 counties in southern Ireland.
Republican	One who aspires to an all-Ireland government by arms with the exclusion of British people in the country.

Roman Catholic	One who holds that the Church is the supreme authority on matters of faith and practice.
RTE	Radio Telefis Eireann.
RUC	Royal Ulster Constabulary. The Police Force of NI from 1 June 1922 until 4 November 2001.
SDLP	Social Democratic and Labour Party.
Secretary of State	Minister appointed by Westminster to oversee the NIO from the introduction of Direct Rule in 1972.
SF	Sinn Fein, a Republican political party.
Shillington's Bridge	A bridge at the lower end of the Garvaghy Road.
SJ	Society of Jesus (Jesuits).
St Andrews Agreement	An attempt in October 2006 to get the NI Assembly to meet again.
Stormont	The NI Parliament from the partition of Ireland in 1921 until 1972.
Superintendent	A high ranking police officer.
TNAG	An Irish language TV channel.
UCB	United Christian Broadcasters.
UDA	Ulster Defence Association – a loyalist paramilitary group founded in 1971 and proscribed in 1992.
UFF	Ulster Freedom Fighters, with close links to UDA.
UTV	Ulster Television.

UUP

Ulster Unionist Party, often called Official Unionist Party, founded in 1905 to maintain the union with Great Britain, composed mostly of Protestants, and was the majority party in Stormont.

UVF

Ulster Volunteer Force, a loyalist paramilitary group.

VE/VJ

Victory Europe/Victory Japan, celebrated the end of World War II in 1945.

Weston Park Talks

An attempt to resolve the political impasse in NI in 2001

BIBLIOGRAPHY

Acheson, Alan — "History of the Church of Ireland, 1691-2001" (Columbia APCK 2002)

Blanchford, Paul — "The Irish and Catholic Power" (1954)

Carrick, Isobel — "Historical Sketch of Drumcree" (1991)

Crooks, D.W. — "Clergy of Derry and Raphoe" (1999)

Crooks, D.W. — "Clergy of Kilmore, Elphin and Ardagh" (2008)

Dixon, Paul — "Northern Ireland" (Palgrave 2001)

Donnan, Hastings — "Culture and Policy of Northern Ireland" (Institute of Irish Studies, QUB 1997)

Dudley-Edwards, Ruth — "The Faithful Tribe" (Harper 1999)

Elliott, Marianne (Ed.) — "The Long Road to Peace in NI" (Liverpool, 2007)

Fleming, W.E.C. — "Armagh Clergy" (2000)

Foster, R.F. — "Luck and the Irish" (Allen Lane, 2007)

Godson, Dean — "Himself Alone – David Trimble" (Harper 2004)

Hennessey, Thomas — "The Northern Ireland Peace Process" (Gill & Macmillan 2000)

Howie, C.G. — "Ezekiel Daniel" (1961)

Jarmin, Neil — "Material Conflicts" (Oxford 1997)

Jess, Mervyn — "The Orange Order" (O'Brien, 2007)

Jones, R. David — "The Orange Citadel" (PCHE, 1996)

Kennaway, Brian — "The Orange Order" (Methuen, 2006)

Lucy, Gordon — "Stand-Off" (USP, 1996)

Mitchell, Haldane — "Images of Omagh" (2000, Vol 8)

McClelland, A. — "The Orange Order" (1997)

McCreary, Alf — "Nobody's Fool. The Life of Archbishop Robin Eames" (Hodder 2004)

Montgomery, G.R. — "The Order on Parade" (GOLI, 1995)

Plowden, Francis — "Orange Societies" (Coyne 1810, Schomberg House Library)

Rankin, F. (Ed.) — "Clergy of Down and Dromore"

Ryder, Chris/Kearney, Vincent — "Drumcree" (Methuen, 2001 & 2002)

Smith, Clifford — "The Vision"

Taylor, J.B. — "Ezekiel" (IVP 1969)

Whitten, J.R. (Ed.) — "The Millennium Book" (GOLI, 2000)

Wolsey, W.H. — "Orangeism in Portadown District" (1935)

INDEX

Surname   *Page number*

A

B

W

Z